Maxine De Shone
1743 W. Lusher Ave.
Elkhart, Indiana
Nov. 11, 1965

KNIT TO FIT

Books by IDA RILEY DUNCAN

THE AMERICAN WOMAN'S COMPLETE SEWING BOOK
THE COMPLETE BOOK OF NEEDLECRAFT
THE COMPLETE BOOK OF PROGRESSIVE KNITTING

KNIT TO FIT

A Comprehensive Guide to
Hand and Machine Knitting

BY

IDA RILEY DUNCAN

Formerly, Assistant Professor, Home Economics Dept.
Wayne State University

LIVERIGHT PUBLISHING CORPORATION
NEW YORK

Library of Congress Catalog Card No. 63-11969

PRINTED IN THE UNITED STATES OF AMERICA

FOREWORD

KNIT TO FIT comprises the material, both hand and machine, from my Progressive School of Knit Design, as well as other pertinent information. My first thought was to leave the projects and answers out of the book because some women and some reviewers might consider it too much like a text book. However, considering the value of the checked answers to my students, I think it is extremely beneficial to retain them.

IDA RILEY DUNCAN

To my late husband, John Brown Duncan.
To my daughters, Peggy and Jean.
To my grandchildren, Shelley, Jock, Dennis,
Lynn, Peter and Jeffrey.

ACKNOWLEDGMENT

I wish to thank my daughter, Peggy, for her assistance with the numerous diagrams, and for her illustrations, without which the book would have little meaning.

CONTENTS

vii

CONTENTS

CONTENTS xiii

KNIT TO FIT

CHAPTER 1

SCIENTIFIC APPROACH TO KNITTING—
HAND AND MACHINE

Too MANY KNITTERS rely upon stereotyped directions with the result that the work is often too big or too small and generally unsatisfactory. In the first place, one may wish to use different yarn and needles, so that the knitting may be tighter or looser than called for. And few of us are a perfect size 12 or 14. Besides, no consideration is given to the style that will bring out the best in the wearer. True, a garment which appears in a knitting manual may be exactly what one wishes, with the exception of the sleeve, or the neckline may emphasize too broad a chin. How simple it can be to change these details, with no guesswork at all!

Just as in the construction of a beautiful piece of architecture, there are principles which may be followed for correct shaping. No graph paper is necessary. Simple diagrams are all that are needed. *The Stitch Gauge* (Chap. 4) and *How to Take Measurements for Knits* (Chap. 3) are very important. Once these are understood, there'll be no cupping of skirts or too-tight garments across the bust, and you will realize that with correct styling, anyone can wear and be very smart in a knit.

It should be stressed here, that this is Ida Riley Duncan's scientific, exclusive formula method. It is hers the world over, so should you discover others using it, you will know it is her method, not theirs. No two individuals could possibly have thought out the same formulas.

No matter what your object is in studying the course, the following four *MUSTS* will aid in your development, either for yourself, in teaching others, or as a designer.

1. Become style conscious
2. Become figure conscious
3. Become color conscious
4. Become personality conscious

From now on, look through magazines and newspapers with a critical eye. Clothes consciousness is easy to acquire this way. Anything that particularly interests you, keep for reference or for file. This does not refer to *Knit Styles* alone, but any style that is adaptable for *Knit* or *Crochet*.

DESIGNING KNITS

If you wish to design or be an instructor of *Knits*, whether for hand or machine, you must learn to diagram and chart directions. You cannot understand or teach others by literally reading a printed page. You yourself must be able to plan a knitted garment, stitch by stitch. There are no stereotyped directions for creative fashion. This, naturally, includes a knowledge of dress design, which is discussed as each special problem is reached in a lesson.

This is a new method, a simple-formula method that will enable you to chart any style or size of garment, using any suitable material, with the assurance that it is going to fit perfectly without any cutting or stretching. And you must realize that any type of garment can be knitted. The only limitations are good taste and the basic rules of design. As stated, there are four *MUSTS* that will aid in your development. Don't miss an opportunity!

American women generally are becoming accustomed to the type and color of clothes which are most becoming, regardless of the dictates of fashion. After you have studied this course, you will be able to diagram and chart clothes that are chic, bring out the good points while concealing the poor, and choose a becoming color. One must remember that style and color have a great effect upon morale. Women should keep their charm and femininity at all times.

Chapters 19 and 20 are on *Color*. They will aid you in becoming Color-Conscious, so read them carefully now at the beginning of the course.

If you own a yarn shop or instruct others, gradually draw diagrams for your customers. Hours of time are saved, not writing but diagramming. Of course, you won't say exactly how you arrived at the figures. And, if you wish to use styles from the knitting manuals, you will be able to change directions to suit individual needs. You will be surprised at the prestige you will gain. Satisfied customers bring other customers.

Later, we shall discuss machine-made garments and why so many look the same, and suggestions as to what may be done to correct this. However, to me, like anything original and custom-made, individual hand-knits have a beauty all their own.

MATERIALS

The study of yarns is very difficult in the United States. In Canada, the British Isles, etc., one knows by the number of folds or plys, the thickness of the yarn. Not so in America. Another confusing thing is that manufacturers and distributors have different names for similar yarns. I suggest you spend some time studying materials in the better shops. Don't become confused. It takes time to know knitting materials.

The following are some of the more general yarns:

Knitting Worsted is a hard-wearing, 4-ply yarn—a good yarn with which to start a beginner. It is suitable for heavier sweaters, mittens, gloves, caps, etc.

Needles. American Standard #5 to #7, aluminum, short, are the easiest to handle.

Double Knitting Worsted. Using #10 needles makes excellent skating or ski sweaters.

Note: If one uses too large needles the garment stretches when washed and a very dissatisfied person is the result. You should never knit more than 6 stitches to the inch when using knitting worsted.

Germantown is a soft, 4-ply yarn, light in weight. It is good for baby blankets, afghans, robes, etc. but too soft for general wear. Use the same needles as for Knitting Worsted.

Sport Yarn is still a worsted yarn and 4-ply but finer than knitting worsted, so the finished product is not as heavy. It is suitable for sportswear of all kinds.

Needles—American Standard #3 to #5.

Saxony may be bought in 2, 3 or 4 ply, but it is often called Baby Yarn. It is extremely soft and suitable for all baby things.

There are countless other yarns, some springy, of all wool, mohair, rayon, wool and nylon, silk, acrilan, straw and many novelty yarns of silky softness, and cool enough for summer wear. Ribbon alone, or with combinations of yarn or metallic, is very fashionable and in this field we are ahead of Paris! It is surprising how ribbons stand wear and look chic for all occasions.

Metallic stripes, beads, sequins, appliqués and embroidery on blouses, sweaters and evening gowns are tremendously popular.

EXCEPTIONS FOR MACHINE-KNITTING

There are certain yarns which are difficult or take more care of on a machine. For example, on closely-needled machines, in order to knit heavier yarn, Knitting Worsted, etc., every other needle has to be used. Nubby yarns are apt to catch if the needle is too tight, and if the yarn is composed of two materials, one springy and the other with no elasticity, the yarn often slips off the needles. Angora yarn must be handled with care because it is so soft, breaks easily and appears flat. Try steaming and shake.

PROJECT

Start your files now both on color and garments.

Note: 1. Project means the work that has to be done in the lesson.

2. When a diagram and chart are asked for, don't look at the answers at the back of the book, where they are explained in detail. Carefully do as the lessons request, *then* check your answers.

Chapter 2

FUNDAMENTALS

You have learned a little about materials. If in doubt about needles for a certain yarn, consult a knitting manual for that type of yarn. If two different sizes are suggested, it is often advisable to use only one size, the intermediate one. Buying two sets of needles as well as the material for a first sweater, adds to the initial cost and may be a deterrent to making one.

Probably you will think that knitting the fundamentals is a waste of time, but you would be surprised at the supposedly experienced knitters who need guidance. In all handwork the workmanship is important, so whether you are going to knit or teach others, you should know what to look for.

PROJECT—Hand-knitting

Make samples of:

1. Garter stitch (all knitting)
2. Stockinette stitch (knit 1 row, purl 1 row)
3. Ribbing (K. 1, P. 1, and K. 2, P. 2)
4. Decreasing and Increasing
5. Binding off

Use sport yarn with #3 or #4 needles. 24 stitches will suffice and about 2 inches in width.

Note: Women who knit the continental way, throwing the thread with the left hand, usually knit more loosely, so I suggest you use one-size smaller needle than the one indicated.

PROJECT—Knitting Machine

1. Stockinette stitch, back and forth on machine.
2. Increasing across a row. It is very time-consuming, means changing the position of many stitches. Often better to change the tension.
3. Increasing at each end. Start where the yarn is attached at the right and wrap the yarn counter clockwise around the next needle. Work a row and add a stitch at the other end, clockwise.
4. Decreasing at both ends. Place the last stitch on the 2nd stitch, then they are knitted as one on the next row.
5. Binding off. Place the first stitch on the second needle, pull the yarn through both stitches. Now have one stitch instead of two. Place this stitch on the next needle and again pull yarn through, and continue in this manner.

Note: When many stitches have to be bound off, and you want a good-looking edge, I consider it better to knit an extra row, then take work from machine. Use an ordinary straight knitting needle, and, taking out one stitch at a time, place the needle in a loop from the back as if to purl. Now bind off the hand way.

6. Joining yarns. Do this at the end if possible, but you may join in the middle. Place the end yarn from the new ball, across the end of attached yarn, and in an opposite direction, so there is an overlap of about 4 inches. Both ends of yarn will be worked in.

Note: Garter Stitch and Moss Stitch are impossible to knit on many machines.

DIAGRAMMING AND CHARTING

Diagramming is a diagram or drawing of each part of the sweater, e.g., back, front and sleeves.
Charting is putting in the necessary figures for the shaping of each part.

So that you will understand the basic shaping for an upper garment, we start with the easiest first—a simple sweater. It would be advisable, if time permits, to knit one, as you learn each change of shaping in the following chapters. It may be a slipover or a cardigan (coat sweater), not shaped at the sides, with any simple neckline (round, turtle, "V" or square), and any type of sleeve (long, short, three-quarter, with fitted cap), with or without buttonholes and pockets and, from your stitch gauge and measurements, for either a man, woman or a child.

In the process you learn to diagram and chart all types of slipovers and cardigans. You can sketch what you desire, or use a picture, or just visualize the style. Absolutely no stereotyped directions are to be used. From the basic shaping of sweaters, you will have good groundwork for the shaping of all upper garments.

See Diagrams 1, 2 and 3.

Slipover

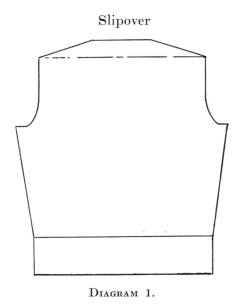

DIAGRAM 1.

Note: I do not advocate knitting small, doll-like garments. The same principles cannot be followed.

Cardigan   Sleeve

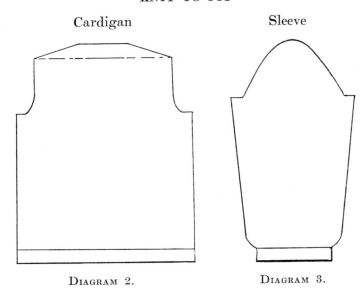

DIAGRAM 2.   DIAGRAM 3.

PROJECT

See **ANSWERS**, Chapter 2, page 222, for possible mistakes in fundamentals.

Note: 1. Actually, the shaping by hand and machine go hand-in-hand. However, in hand-knitting, there are both straight and circular needles, whereas circular knitting is found only in very expensive knitting machines. Even there, there are limitations for both circular and straight-needled knitting machines. The main thing is to design the best way possible first, then, if necessary, change the directions to suit the particular machine you wish to operate.

2. Some machines have no ribbers, or they are expensive, and, for personal use, easy to do without. Simulated ribbing will suffice, or a stitch may be dropped and picked up with the tool or crochet hook, the correct way; but I feel that if one wishes to get away from the cheaper machine look, especially around necklines, etc., it is better to rib by hand.

CHAPTER 3

MEASUREMENTS FOR KNITS

THE BODY MEASUREMENTS given in many knitting manuals are very confusing. It is not body measurements one needs for knit design but the necessary measurements of the finished garment for a particular person. No blocking will ever stop a skirt from cupping if the necessary width has not been added at the hips.

The following measurements are those one usually sees:

Women's and Misses' Body Measurements

Size	12	14	16	18	20
Bust	30	32	34	36	38
Waist	25	26½	28	30	32
Hip	33	35	37	39	41
Arm Length	16½	17	17½	18	18

A size 14 is 32 inches around the bust. It isn't a bra' measurement that we require. We don't want to stretch to fit, but work to the finished garment measurements. When a designer designs clothes, she adds the necessary fulness to suit the requirements of the individual, the style of garment and the type of material.

HOW TO TAKE MEASUREMENTS

Note: Never try to take your own measurements.

Waist

(a) If there is difficulty in locating the position of the waist, it is just below the ribs and easy to locate if one bends sideways.

(b) In a large figure where the abdomen is raised in the

9

corset, the actual waist is not used in front. Lower the tape ½ inch or 1 inch as necessity demands.

This measurement should be taken with two fingers between the body and the tape measure. This does not mean that it should be taken loosely, but the tape may be moved around the waist easily, not tightly.

Bust

The position of the bust varies with the individual. It may be two inches below the armpit in young figures, or four inches or more for some adults. This measurement is taken exactly around the fullest part. The tape is not raised at the back. Knitting is worked straight, horizontally.

Note: This measurement is the one used when buying a bra' or a pattern and is not the one used for the finished garment. This measurement is taken as a guide for the next two.

To find the necessary bust measurement, the across-the-back underarm measurement and the front bust measurement are required.

Across-the-Back Underarm

Raise and bend arms slightly towards the front. Don't raise arms too high. Find the mid-point of the hollow which comes immediately under the tip of the shoulder and measure across the back, from hollow to hollow where the underarm seams should be.

See Illustration 1.

Front Bust Measurement

This is taken across the largest part of the bust in a horizontal line from underarm to underarm seam and loose enough to allow flat fingers under the tape.

Total Bust Measurement

The *back* and *front combined measurements* are the necessary total *bust* measurement. Check this measurement by adding 4 inches to the previous bust measurement and it will give

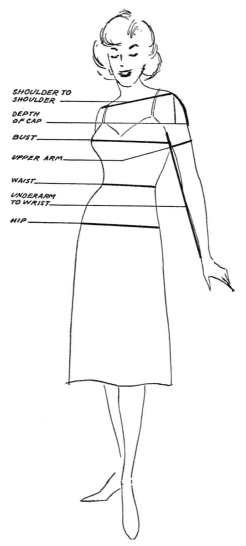

SHOULDER TO
SHOULDER

DEPTH
OF CAP

BUST

UPPER ARM

WAIST

UNDERARM
TO WRIST

HIP

ILLUSTRATION 1.

you the *least* your combined bust measurement should measure for any knitted sweater.

Note: (a) Under no conditions should the back underarm measurement be larger than the front measurement.

(b) Contrary to belief, on a normal figure there isn't a great deal of difference in these measurements, even for a woman. One must allow for freedom of movement at the back.

(c) The combined measurement must be at least 4 inches more than a bra' or normal bust measurement, adding 1 inch for B cup, 2 inches for C and so on, to actual bra' measurement.

Waist to Underarm

If the tape is fastened around the waist, it will aid in taking the correct measurement. This is taken from the hollow of the armpit (don't raise the arms too high) to the center of the tape around the waist. This would be too long for armholes for fitted caps of sleeves, so deduct 1 inch from this measurement and the deducted measurement is the one used. (No sleeve fits close to the armpit.)

Shoulder to Shoulder

I consider this a very important measurement. There is nothing worse than drooping shoulders. Raise an arm and feel the shoulder tip at the very top—just before the slope. Measure across the shoulders at the back from the small bone that marks the tip of one shoulder to the other. See illustration.

Note: When taking a child's shoulder measurement, multiply the inches by two. If the answer is almost the necessary chest measurement, you will know it is too big. There must be sufficient stitches to take off at the underarm.

Wrist

This measurement is taken below the wrist bone toward the hand and is taken exactly.

Upperarm

As the largest part of the upperarm varies with the individual, measure the fullest part and take it exactly. Don't add anything. This applies to a child too. The width is taken care of when we come to sleeves.

Forearm

This is the fullest part between the wrist and the elbow. It is only necessary for women with large forearms and for men. It should be taken exactly.

Sleeve Underarm Length

The arm should be raised a little. This measurement is taken from the underarm mid-point, the hollow at the armpit, down the arm to the wrist, on a line with the thumb. One inch is deducted from this measurement, as for the waist to underarm measurement. This is the one used for the sleeve length.

Armhole or Armscye

The armhole or armscye is the closed curve starting from the shoulder tip, passing around and under the arm and back to the shoulder tip again. Many armholes, especially in larger, cheaper clothes are too large, giving an ugly fit in front, or they may be too small in garments for smaller sizes, especially if one perspires. Try to take this measurement, then test your ability with the following rule.

An armhole curve should be at least seven or eight inches more than the upper-arm measurement, never less, according to the needs of the wearer. For an adult, this means that if the exact upper-arm measurement is 11 inches, the curve of the armhole must measure 18 or 19 inches. Whether you add 7 or 8 inches is a matter for you to decide.

These are all the necessary measurements for the first project, a sweater. To test your ability, measure a man, a woman and a child and write the answers on the chart.

CHART

                                        MAN   WOMAN   CHILD

Waist
Bust or Chest (Straight Measurement)
Across the Back Underarm
Front Bust or Chest Measurement
Back and Front Bust Measurements
   Combined
Waist to Underarm
Shoulder to Shoulder
Wrist
Upperarm
Forearm
Sleeve Underarm Length
Armhole or Armscye

Note: If the combined back and front bust or chest measurements and the shoulder-to-shoulder measurements are taken correctly, there should only be about 1 inch of stitches to be bound off at the beginning of the armhole shaping, for an adult.

CHAPTER 4

IMPORTANCE OF A CORRECT STITCH GAUGE

THE STITCH GAUGE is the name given to the number of stitches to the inch and rows to the inch that are measured on a piece of stockinette stitch. The gauge depends upon the material knitted, the size of the needles and how a person knits, or the material and the suitable tension of the machine.

TAKING A GAUGE

Why so much difficulty has been encountered in the *fit* of *knits* is partly because of an inaccurate stitch gauge and partly because of not knowing how to take necessary measurements. Both are equally important. Remember, when diagramming, the final necessary measurements are to be used. Therefore, the stitch gauge will be the same as when the garment is worn. To become accustomed to the small amount of stretch the material will have when it is flattened, takes practice, but this does come.

At the beginning, I advise steaming the piece of fabric. This does not mean that one should pin it down, in which case it could be pinned to many sizes. Simply steam over the piece, on the wrong side, using a damp cloth and a medium hot iron, or no cloth and a steam iron, *keeping the weight of the iron in the hand*. Now it will be the same as the fabric in the completed garment.

KNITTING THE SAMPLE PIECE OF MATERIAL
FOR THE STITCH GAUGE

With the yarn and the needles that are to be used for the garment, cast on 24 stitches and knit a piece of stockinette stitch (knit one row, purl one row) for about 2½ inches.

15

Note: 1. For thicker material, fewer stitches are necessary.

2. The heavier the yarn, the greater an error can be.

Method

(a) Steam the piece of material.

(b) Count the number of stitches and rows to the inch, as in the diagram. A linen tape is the best. Do not measure the loops on the needle but in the center of the work. Do this several times, over 1 inch, then 2. Remember, ½ a stitch makes a big difference when measuring stitches to the inch. For example, a piece of material 12 inches long, 6 stitches to the inch, requires 72 stitches. But 12 inches at 6½ stitches to the inch, needs 78 stitches—a difference of 6 stitches which is important in the fit of a garment. *See diagram.*

(c) Use stockinette stitch for the gauge of any texture stitch.

Note: The same method is used when making a gauge on a machine.

TYPE OF SWEATER

By this time, you should have decided what type of basic sweater you wish to knit, or diagram, if you are busy. Use a sketch, a photograph or visualize the style. It must be a *basic* sweater not an evening one, fitted at the sides. These come later. This is a learning process and no matter how adept you are at knitting, use ribbing and stockinette stitch for the back of the sweater. No fancy stitches. Knit from your diagram. The main things are that your lines are clear and your figures accurate. No written explanations are necessary.

If you don't own a yarn shop, buy your material from a reputable store. The knitting manuals for that particular brand will tell you the amount and size of needles. There are many "no dye lot" sweater yarns on the market and I suggest these, because one need not buy all at one time and, if one intends to go into business, sometimes it is a good selling point.

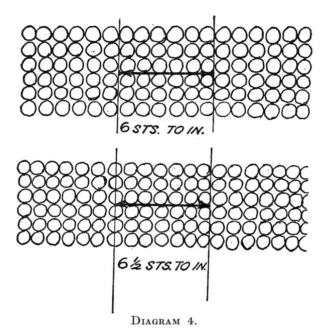

6 STS. TO IN.

6 ½ STS. TO IN.

DIAGRAM 4.

Important to Machine Knitters

As binding off is much more difficult and time-consuming than adding stitches on a machine, it is easier to begin at the top and knit down, so wait until you understand all the back shaping before you begin, or try both ways to test the time and ease.

CHAPTER 5

KNITTING OF GARMENTS—SWEATERS

DIFFERENCES BETWEEN MACHINE, HAND-LOOMED AND HAND-KNIT

MACHINE KNITS, as the name implies, are manufactured by a machine but there are differences in machine knits.

(a) The material is knitted on a machine, then the pieces are marked from a pattern, sewn before cutting so the pieces don't fray, cut and sewn together.

(b) The pieces are shaped on a machine, using different techniques to adjust the shaping. These are a better kind.

Note: If you ask your friends about the wearability of cheaper machine knits, you will learn that they are not satisfactory. They sag and grow long. But there is still another very important factor. They are "much of a muchness." The same type of neckline, the same short sleeves and the same narrow ribbed skirt.

It should be understood by those who have knitting machines that when making or designing machine knits, one must consider the design of hand-knits first, where all the shaping may be accomplished according to the rules of good dress design. Then the directions have to be adjusted according to the limitations of your machine.

Hand-loomed is rather an ambiguous cognomen. These are machine-knit garments, finished by hand, and possess more originality and style than cheaper machine knits.

Note: Pay special attention to these facts and keep away from the cheap machine-made look.

Hand-knit as the name implies, means that the garment has been knitted entirely by hand. If a hand-knitted garment has been designed and charted correctly, it should fit perfectly without any stretching, shrinking or cutting. I, myself, can chart any garment, for any figure, from the stitch gauge of an experienced knitter, with the assurance that it will not require a fitting. This is to be your aim.

BASIC PRINCIPLES OF DESIGN FOR SWEATERS
WITH SIMPLE LINES
Diagramming and Charting any Size *Slipover* or *Cardigan* with any Type of Yarn

Slipover Sweater (slip over the head)

Note: 1. Simple sweaters are made the same width at the front as the back unless the person has an unusually large bust. However, a woman with a large bust should never wear a slip-over sweater.

2. Two sets of different sized needles are not necessary for knitting a sweater. It is advisable to increase at the waist rather than use needles two sizes larger. But, if smaller needles are desired for the ribbing, make a stitch gauge with the larger ones and figure the number of stitches necessary for the bust, then use the same number of stitches with the smaller needles for the ribbing.

3. Your work should be knitted neither too tightly nor too loosely. Knitted sweaters should be washable. If knitted too loosely, they sag; if fitted too tightly, they mat.

The following woman's measurements are the ones we shall use for the examples throughout the sweater lessons.

1.	Waist	28	inches
2.	Across the Back Underarm	17½	”
3.	Front Bust Measurement	18½	”
4.	Total Bust Measurement	36	”
5.	Wrist	6	”
6.	Upperarm	11	”
7.	Forearm	9	”
8.	Sleeve Underarm Length	18	”
9.	Armhole or Armscye	18	”

Stitch Gauge—6 stitches to the inch
8 rows to the inch

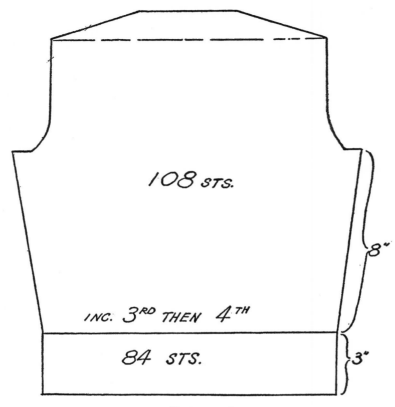

DIAGRAM 5.

BACK

Method

1. Waist Band or Ribbing—worn below the waist.

The waist is 28 inches. Half of this is 14 inches to be multiplied by the stitch gauge, 6 stitches to the inch. 14 times 6 is 84 stitches, which is divisible by 4, for K. 2, P. 2. If not divisible by 4, take the nearest number that is. Whether to use K. 2, P. 2, or K. 1, P. 1, depends upon the type of yarn. For heavier yarn, use K. 2, P. 2, but it is advisable that a beginner always knit K. 2, P. 2, for ribbing.

The ribbing is generally 3 inches or more for adults, and 2 inches for a child. Be sure to stretch to the correct width before measuring.

2. Body of the sweater.

Note: The fronts and backs of basic sweaters are always the same width.

The necessary bust measurement is 36 inches, ½ of 36 is 18 inches. 18 × 6 stitches to the inch is 108 stitches.

ADDING STITCHES

In basic sweaters, all the stitches are added on the first row after the ribbing, and added evenly across the row on the right side of the work.

Method

1. The number of stitches for ½ the waist is 84 stitches, and ½ the bust is 108 stitches, a difference of 24 stitches.
2. Take the number of stitches to be added into the number of stitches to be increased. For example, to add 12 stitches to 72; 12 goes into 72—6 times, therefore increase in every 6th stitch. If the number doesn't go in evenly, don't increase in the stitches that are left over.
3. In our example, we divide 24 into 84 which goes 3½ times, or 2 in 7 stitches; so, we increase first in the 3rd stitch, then in the 4th across the row and purl back. Work stockinette stitch for 8 inches, which is the underarm to waist measurement.

Method for Figuring Body Stitches

1. ½ the waist measurement multiplied by the stitch gauge is the number of stitches for ½ the waist.
2. ½ the bust or chest measurement multiplied by the stitch gauge gives the number of stitches for across the back.

3. The difference between the stitches for ½ the bust and ½ the waist equals the number of stitches to be added.

Note: The same principles apply to a man's, woman's or child's sweater.

PROJECT

1. Diagram and chart your own sample sweater to the armhole.
2. Knit your own sweater to the armhole.

CHAPTER 6

CARDIGAN OR COAT SWEATER

BACK

1. A SIMPLE cardigan or coat sweater is knitted straight to the underarm, using half the bust or chest measurement for the back. If the hips are larger than the chest measurement, say 46 inches for the hips and 42 inches for the chest, a medium measurement should be used—44 inches. No cardigan should be larger at the hips than at the chest.

2. A narrow band should be used at the bottom of a cardigan, about one and a half inches wide, or actually it should be the front band width, unless you are making a sweater that fits at the waist. A wide band gives added width at the hips. It may be of K. 1, P. 1, garter or seed stitch, etc.

The length of a cardigan depends upon the figure of the wearer. It should not stop just above a protruding derrière. Mark the proposed length and stand back for judgment— should not be too long for a short person as she would appear all body and not too long for a tall person either. She would appear taller.

Diagram 6 is self-explanatory.

EXPERIENCE IN DIAGRAMMING AND CHARTING

If you wish to have experience in diagramming and charting both a slipover and a cardigan, use the following measurements. They are not standard but are a man's and woman's measurements, taken as they should be for knitting or crochet. Few of us are a perfect 12 or 14. We must learn to cope with the

23

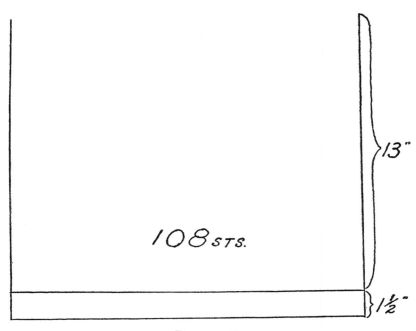

DIAGRAM 6.

irregularities of form, so that our garments are not too tight in one place or too large in another.

Gauge—6 stitches to the inch—man
       7 stitches to the inch—woman

	MAN		WOMAN	
Waist	38	inches	28	inches
Across Back Underarm	21	"	17½	"
Front Bust or Chest	21	"	18½	"
Chest or Bust	42	"	36	"
Waist to Underarm	11	"	8	"
Shoulder to Shoulder	17	"	14½	"
Wrist	8	"	6	"
Upperarm	13	"	11	"
Sleeve Underarm Length	20	"	17½	"
Armhole or Armscye	21	"	19	"

In all diagramming and charting, no graph paper is necessary. Become accustomed to drawing diagrams. They may look very amateurish at first, but you will be surprised how you will progress with a little determination. Think nothing is impossible if you make up your mind.

PROJECTS

1. Diagram and chart to the armhole, the back of the man's slipover and cardigan.
2. Diagram and chart to the armhole, the back of the woman's slipover and cardigan.

    You may wonder why you are diagramming both slipover and cardigan, when they have apparently the same figures. There is a reason, which we shall learn later.
3. Check your answers on pages 222 to 225.

CHAPTER 7

SHAPING OF ARMHOLE OR ARMSCYE

It isn't too many years ago that the shaping of an armhole was a complicated procedure. Fashion design today is much more simple yet beautiful. One might compare modern dress design with modern furniture design, functional, simple and of easy construction.

I wonder if you have noticed that many armholes in knits are too small. From actual experience, I have learned that a 10-inch to a 12-inch upperarm is the average size of a young adult, more, for many older women. Naturally, the size of the armhole should be proportionate to the size of the upperarm.

METHOD FOR FIGURING THE SIZE OF ARMHOLES

A 10-inch upperarm requires from 17 to 18 inches for the armhole curve—fitted cap.

An 11-inch upperarm requires from 18 to 19 inches for the armhole curve—fitted cap.

A 12-inch upperarm requires from 19 to 20 inches for the armhole curve—fitted cap,
and so on for larger upperarms.

Note: Throughout the course, when considering the differences for a child, allow ¾ of what was considered for an adult, therefore, 5½ to 6 inches should be added to the upperarm for a child's armhole curve.

Measuring Armhole

If the total armhole measurement is 18 inches, half the armhole curve is 9 inches, *measuring around the curve to the tip of the shoulder.*

Shaping Armhole

Follow diagrams. The shoulder to shoulder measurement is 14 inches. 14 times 6 stitches to the inch is 84 stitches. This is an even number. Make it even if it doesn't work out that way. Always use even numbers in knitting.

SLIPOVER

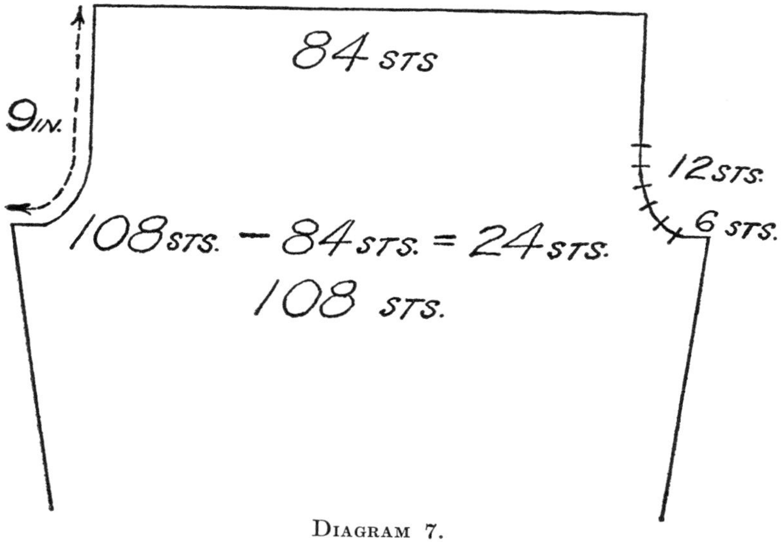

DIAGRAM 7.

The difference between the stitches required for the shoulder, 84 stitches, and the number of stitches for the across the back underarm, 108 stitches, is 24 stitches, to be taken off at both sides of the armholes. 12 stitches to be taken off for each. We bind off half the total number of stitches at the beginning, then the remainder are reduced by knitting 2 together at the beginning and end of every front row.

As we can only bind off at the beginning of rows, we bind off half of the 12 stitches, which is 6 stitches, at the beginning of the next two rows, then knit 2 together at the beginning and

end of the next 6 knitted rows, until the shoulder stitches remain, 84 stitches.

Work even in stockinette stitch until half the armhole measurement is knitted, which is 9 inches, measuring around.

Note: If the number is uneven, say 15 stitches, divide the
number by 2 and allow the extra stitch to be bound off at first—
8 stitches bound off and knit 2 together, 7 times.

CARDIGAN

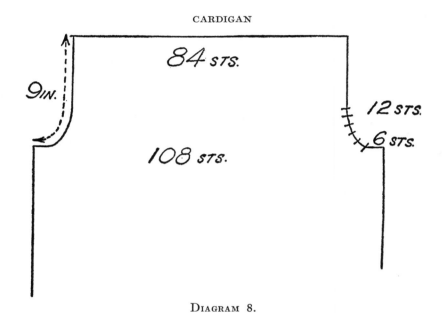

DIAGRAM 8.

FORMULA FOR SHAPING ARMHOLES

1. Bind off ½ the total number of stitches at the beginning
of the next 2 rows, then knit 2 together at the beginning and
end of the knitted rows, until the total number of stitches has
been reduced.

2. Work even until ½ the armhole measurement is knitted.

Note for Machine: Sometimes we are unable to measure around so take ½ the total measurement for a man or a woman and deduct 1½ inches, and for a child, 1 to 1¼ inches straight from the first bind off, and count the number of rows per inch.

PROJECTS

1. Diagram and chart the armholes of the 4 examples on page 225.
2. Diagram your own sweater to the tip of the shoulder, ready for the shaping of the shoulders.
3. Check the answers on pages 225 and 226.

CHAPTER 8

OPENINGS AT THE BACK

Do you understand the method of shaping so far? You shouldn't pass to the next step unless the preceding steps are clear in your mind.

Back openings are very smart for certain figures (straight backs) but they should be taboo for older persons, especially if one has a "dowager hump," as it is called. Openings, buttons, etc., attract attention and any figure discrepancies should be camouflaged, if possible, not pointed out.

TO START THE OPENING AT THE BACK

An opening generally begins immediately after the stitches for the armhole have been decreased, or approximately two inches up from the first bind off.

(a) Knit across to the center.

(b) Place the remaining half of the stitches on a stitch holder or a safety-pin. The back is worked in two separate pieces.

(c) Continue the right side until the tip of the shoulder is reached.

(d) Shape the shoulder and neckline.

(e) The left side is completed the same as the right in reverse.

(f) The opening may be single crocheted and loops of chain stitch used as buttonholes. This is done after the garment is put together.

Note: All change of shaping is done on the right side of the work with the exception of binding off, which cannot be done

30

at the end of a row, so this and only this, is done on the wrong side of the work. The knit 2 together decreases are always worked on the right side at the very edge; and if these rules are remembered, no confusion can arise either at the armholes, shoulders, necklines, etc.

MACHINE KNITTERS

To Start the Opening at the Back

In order to work the 2 pieces separately and at the same time, 2 balls of yarn are necessary.

(a) Knit across to the center.

(b) Use the second ball for the other half, and work back and forth on both sides until the tips of the shoulders are reached.

(c) The left shoulder is bound off the same as the right in reverse.

(d) Bind off all the stitches for the back of the neck.

FULL-FASHIONED SWEATERS

The word full-fashioned, with regard to sweaters, is very misleading. It simply means that the decreases show, both on the armholes and caps of the sleeves. Strictly, from the point of view of design, they are not correct, because any change of shaping takes place in the seam—whoever thought of drawing attention to a seam in a sewn garment? Also, there should be a certain number of stitches bound off at the underarm. All garment shaping should conform to the contour of the body. However, if one wishes a full-fashioned effect, find the number of stitches to be decreased, the same as previously, then decrease by knitting 2 together, at the beginning and end of every 4th row, 5 stitches in, until all the necessary stitches have been reduced.

CHAPTER 9

HOW TO SHAPE SHOULDERS

THE CORRECT FIT of shoulders has a great effect upon the fit of the upper part of the sleeves, the neckline and the bust. I suggest for knits that you never have anything extreme and always a shoulder line that suits the individual. Think of a woman, heavy below the waist, small bust in comparison and sloping shoulders. She definitely needs her shoulders slightly padded, even in a knit. Yes, and she can wear a knit if it is correctly styled. On the other hand, if the shoulders appear too broad for small hips, the shoulders should never be padded, no matter what the fashion. A raglan sleeve would be the best for her.

BASIC SHAPING FOR SHOULDERS USING DIFFERENT STITCH GAUGES

Shoulder lines are sloped to conform to the shape of the shoulder. Allow one third of the total number of shoulder to shoulder stitches for each shoulder and one third for the back of the neck. Never have fewer stitches for the back of the neck than the shoulder.

Follow diagram 9; ⅓ of 84 stitches is 28 stitches for each shoulder and 28 stitches for the back of the neck.

IMPORTANCE OF THE STITCH GAUGE FOR SHAPING SHOULDERS

A few explanations are necessary, so you understand why so many steps are used for certain stitch gauges. Strange as it may seem, women's shoulders are straighter and broader than they were twenty years ago. Approximately a slope of one inch is the best for all purposes.

The following stitch gauges may be used for the shaping:
For 6 stitches to the inch there are 8 rows to the inch.
For 7 stitches to the inch there are 10 rows to the inch.

For 8 stitches to the inch there are 12 rows to the inch, and so on.

As we are only able to bind off at the beginning of rows, and 6 stitches to the inch has 8 rows, half of the 8 rows, 4, must be the number of times we are able to bind off at one end and 4 times at the other. For 7 stitches to the inch, there are 10 rows, so 5 are the number of times that we bind off the allotted stitches for the shoulder. 8 stitches to the inch, which have 12 rows, require 6. Follow diagrams.

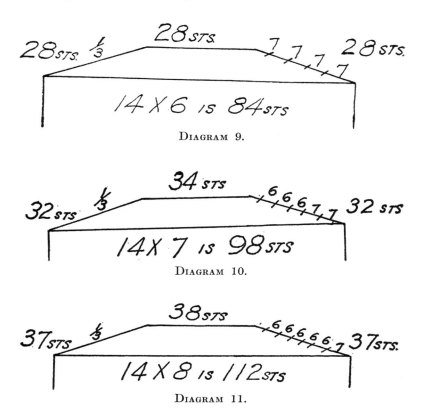

DIAGRAM 9.

DIAGRAM 10.

DIAGRAM 11.

Note: (a) If the stitch gauge is 6½ stitches to the inch, I would consider it 7 and use 5 slopes for each shoulder.

(b) If the number doesn't go evenly into the stitches for the shoulder, allow the extra stitches for the slopes nearest the shoulder.

In diagram 9, the stitch gauge is 6 stitches to the inch, so 28 is divided by 4, which means that 7 stitches are bound off, 4 times on each shoulder, making 8 rows altogether.

Method for Shoulder Shaping

1. One-third of the stitches are used for each shoulder and one-third for the back of the neck.
2. Shape each shoulder in, from 3 to 7 slopes, depending upon the stitch gauge.

5 stitches to the inch	3 slopes
6 stitches to the inch	4 "
7 stitches to the inch	5 "
8 stitches to the inch	6 "
and so on.	

Note carefully! For a high, round neckline slipover, without any opening—this also means a turtle neck—the one third neck opening isn't large enough for the head to pass through, so do not bind off the last step on each side but add these stitches to the back of the neck.

Study diagrams carefully.
6 stitches to the inch—4 slopes

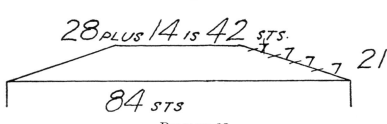

DIAGRAM 12.

7 stitches to the inch—5 slopes

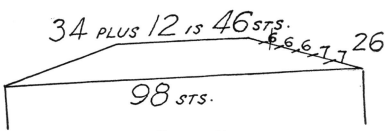

DIAGRAM 13.

8 stitches to the inch—6 slopes

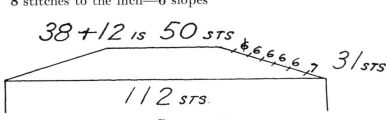

DIAGRAM 14.

Note: When the stitch gauge is 5 stitches to the inch or under, deduct 1 inch of stitches from each of the last slopes and add the 2 inches to the back of the neck stitches. The neck opening would be too large if the last slope were used.

HOW TO FIGURE THE BACK IF WORKING FROM THE TOP DOWN

Note: This method is easier for machine-knitters.

We shall use the following measurements:
Waist—28 inches.
Bust—36 inches.
Underarm to Waist—8 inches.
Shoulder to Shoulder—14 inches.
Armhole—18 inches.
Stitch Gauge or Tension—6 stitches to the inch, 8 rows to the inch. *See Diagram 9.*

For either a cardigan or slipover, except for a high round neck, cast on 28 stitches for the back of the neck. For a high round-neck slipover, cast on 28 stitches plus 2 times 7, which is 14, making 42 stitches. Add 7 stitches at each end, every other row, until 84 stitches. Work even until the shaping for the armhole. 7½ inches × 8 rows to the inch equals 60 rows. But the diagram shows 6 decreases of knit 2 together, every other row, making 12 rows. 60 rows minus 12 rows is 48 rows. Therefore work 48 rows even, then shape the armholes, until 108 stitches.

The underarm to waist is 8 inches, at 8 rows to the inch is 64 rows to the waist.

For the ribbing, decrease to 84 stitches, or change the tension, or place the stitches on straight needles and work by hand.

PROJECT

1. Diagram and chart the shoulders of the man's and woman's example sweaters as follows:

    (a) Slipover sweater
    1. Shoulders for either a "V", square or oval neckline.
    2. Shoulders for high, round neckline.

    (b) Cardigan
    Shoulders for cardigan of general styling.

2. Test your answers on pages 227 to 229.

CHAPTER 10

HOW TO COMPLETE THE BACK OF
A SWEATER

COMPLETING THE BACK OF THE NECK ACCORDING TO THE TYPE OF SWEATER

1. SLIPOVER SWEATERS.

FOR slipover sweaters without an opening either at the front or at the back, do not bind off the back of the neck, no matter what type of neckline in front, if ribbing is to be used around the neckline.

If ribbing is desired, knit the same rib as for the waist [one would never put two different designs of lace on a blouse] K. 2, P. 2, or K. 1, P. 1, as the case may be. One inch is generally the width. Be sure to bind off loosely (as elastic as the rest of the work) knitting the knits, and purling the purls, as you bind off.

2. CARDIGANS OR COAT SWEATERS.

a. Round Necklines

The back of the neck is bound off loosely and the stitches picked up all around the neckline after the sweater is put together.

b. "V" Necklines

The same band that is used up the front is continued around the neck, then the ends woven together either at the back of the neck or at a shoulder seam.

TO CHECK THE STITCH GAUGE

Check the Stitch Gauge of your completed back. Is it the same as when you started? An experienced knitter will not change, but a beginner's gauge must be checked.

37

HOW TO RECTIFY CHANGE IN STITCH GAUGE

Generally, a beginning knitter knits tighter as she progresses, because she gradually learns to throw her thread correctly. This means that the stitch gauge should be checked towards the armhole or armscye, if possible. If she has tightened her work, figure the necessary number of stitches from her new gauge for the shoulders. It is so important that shoulders fit.

TO LEARN THE NECESSARY NUMBER OF STITCHES FOR THE FRONT BUST MEASUREMENT

Example: Bust—38 inches.
First stitch gauge—6½ stitches to the inch.
Second stitch gauge—7 stitches to the inch.

Multiply the total bust measurement by the new gauge. 38 times 7 stitches to the inch is 266 stitches. 19 inches times 6½ stitches is 124 stitches for the back. Subtract the back stitches from the total stitches, which is 142 for the front bust.

PROJECT

Diagram the shoulders of your own sweater and complete the back according to the type desired.

TEXTURE STITCHES, HAND AND MACHINE

ARE YOU GOING to use a different stitch for your sweater in the front? I mean a texture stitch, not a lace-pattern. What are texture stitches? The texture of cloth means the surface quality or how it looks on top, or in knitting, the way the knits and purls are placed. Some of the texture stitches have no influence upon the apparent size of a person, while others possess a slimming effect (diagonal patterns), and some make a person look larger. Cable stitches, with their bulk, have a tendency to increase breadth, but if they are used sparingly, in the form of up and down stripes, they add length.

TEXTURE STITCHES BY HAND

#1. *Pebble Rib*
Multiple of 2 stitches

Row 1: * K. 1, P. 1, repeat from * across the row.
Row 2: Purl.

ILLUSTRATION 2.

Note: The next pattern has a multiple of 6 stitches plus 3 stitches. That means that each pattern requires 6 stitches, so if 3 patterns were used, 18 stitches would be necessary, plus 3 stitches for the beginning and end of the row, 21 stitches altogether.

#2.
Multiple of 6 sts plus 3

Row 1: K. 1, * P. 1, K. 5, repeat from * ending P. 1, K. 1.
Row 2: K. 1, * P. 1, K. 1, P. 3, K. 1., repeat from * ending P. 1, K. 1.
Row 3: K. 1, * K. 2, P. 1, K. 1, P. 1, K. 1, repeat from * ending K. 2.
Row 4: K. 1, * P. 3, K. 1, P. 2, repeat from * ending P. 1, K. 1.

Repeat the 4 rows for pattern.

ILLUSTRATION 3.

#3. *Multiple of 7 plus 5*

Row 1: Knit.
Row 2: Purl.

Row 3: K. 1, * K. 3, P. 4, repeat from * ending K. 4.
Row 4: K. 1, * P. 3, K. 4, repeat from * ending P. 3, K. 1.
Repeat the 4 rows.

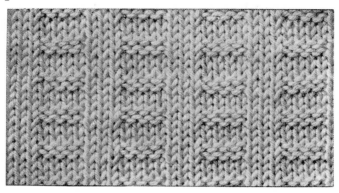

ILLUSTRATION 4.

#4. *Multiple of 4 plus 3*

Row 1: K. 1, * K. 1, P. 3, repeat from * ending K. 2.
Row 2: K. 1, * P. 2, K. 2, repeat from * ending P. 1, K. 1.
Row 3: K. 1, * K. 1, P. 1, K. 2, repeat from * ending K. 2.
Row 4: Purl.
Repeat the 4 rows.

ILLUSTRATION 5.

#5. *Multiple of 6 plus 2*

> *Rows 1 and 5:* * P. 2, K. 4, repeat from * ending P. 2.
> *Rows 2 and 4:* * K. 2, P. 4, repeat from * ending K. 2.
> *Rows 5 and 7:* * P. 3, K. 2, P. 1, repeat from * ending P. 2.
> *Rows 6 and 8:* * K. 3, P. 2, K. 1, repeat from * ending K. 2.
> *Row 9:* Purl.
> *Row 10:* Knit.

Repeat 10 rows for pattern.

ILLUSTRATION 6.

#6. *Cable*
Multiple of 8 plus 6

> *Row 1:* K. 1, * K. 4, P. 4, repeat from * ending K. 5.
> *Row 2:* P. 1, * P. 4, K. 4, repeat from * ending P. 5.
> *Rows 3 and 4:* Repeat rows 1 and 2.
> *Row 5:* K. 1. * With double pointed needle slip the next 2 stitches on to it, from the back, knit the next 2 stitches, then knit 2 stitches on the double pointed needle, P. 4, * ending K. 5.
> *Row 6:* Same as Row 2.

Repeat the 6 rows.

ILLUSTRATION 7.

Note: Extra stitches have to be allowed for cables as they tighten the work. 2 extra stitches are necessary for each. That means that if 5 cables are used, 10 extra stitches should be added on the first row after the ribbing, as well as the necessary stitches for the bust. However, the diagramming is the same as without the cables, reducing 2 stitches at every cable when a change of shaping is made.

BUTTONHOLES (Hand)

The most important buttonhole is the neck buttonhole. If ribbing is going to be used at the neck edge, this should be 1 inch deep and the buttonhole placed in the center. If a cardigan is fitted at the waist and the ribbing is 3 inches wide, work 2 buttonholes in the ribbing, 1 inch apart, and the rest 2 to 2½ inches.

To Knit Buttonholes

Bind off the necessary number of stitches on the right side and knit across the row. On the wrong side, purl to where the stitches are bound off—this is where many have difficulty— now turn the work to add the stitches which are knitted on. Knit into the stitch on the left hand needle; don't take off the loop, but turn the stitch just made and place it on the left hand needle. Add the same number of stitches that were bound off, then again turn the work and purl to the end.

Finish each buttonhole with buttonhole stitch after the garment has been completed.

TEXTURE STITCHES FOR MACHINE

1. *Different Tension*

A number of rows are knitted with a loose stitch or different tension.

a. Work 13 rows with the tension set at 4.
b. Work 8 rows with the tension set at 10.

ILLUSTRATION 8.

2. *Skipped Stitches*

The needles are put out of service at certain distances from each other.

a. Put every second needle out of service.
b. Knit in the usual way.

Note: Some machines won't take thick yarn using every needle, then every second stitch is used.

ILLUSTRATION 9.

3. *Resting Position*

a. Work 3 rows.
b. Raise every 3rd needle into resting position.
c. Work 4 rows.
d. Bring resting needles back into working position.

Repeat the 4 steps.

ILLUSTRATION 10.

4. *Crossed Stitches*

Two consecutive stitches are crossed at regular intervals.

a. Knit 6 rows.

b. By means of tools, cross stitches 13 and 14, 19 and 20, 25 and 26, always leaving 4 knit stitches between.

c. Repeat a and b, alternating pattern as in illustration.

ILLUSTRATION 11.

5. *Cables*

There may be 4, 6 or 8 stitches in each cable. Change the position of half the stitches, so the first half is knitted last, and vice versa.

For example, if there are 4 stitches for the cable, hook the cable tools on the first 2 and last 2 needles, keeping the tools parallel to the needles. Cross them, then replace the stitches on the needles beneath the open latch.

See Hand Cables on page 42.

BUTTONHOLES BY MACHINE

1. Using separate piece of yarn

a. Lay a contrasting piece of yarn in the heads of the needles where buttonhole is going to be made.

  b. Push the needles back to working position and continue knitting back and forth.
  c. When work is completed, pull out the separate length of yarn, leaving unlocked stitches.
  d. Stitch around by hand and finish with buttonhole stitch.

2. This is somewhat like a hand-knitted buttonhole.

  a. Rest all needles except those that come ahead of the buttonhole.
  b. Knit to the buttonhole and rest the stitches just made.
  c. Bind off the stitches for the buttonhole, ending with 2 stitches on one needle.
  d. Place all the needles in working position and knit one row.
  e. Work back to the buttonhole and cast on the same number of stitches as were bound off.
  f. Work the rest of the row.

PROJECT

Knit samples of cables and buttonholes.

CHAPTER 12

FRONTS OF SWEATERS

SLIPOVER

THE FRONT of a slipover is knitted the same as the back until the front neckline is reached. The extra length that is sometimes added to the underarm to waist-length in front for a woman, takes the place of a dart, which is often used when sewing. In knitting, it is eased into the seam, 2 to 4 inches below the underarm. For general purposes, extra length isn't necessary, but use your own discretion, whether ½ an inch or 1 inch should be added.

CARDIGAN

As the position of the buttonholes is important, the side on which the buttons are fastened is knitted first. Therefore, for a woman's garment, it is the left side and for a man's, the right. The general rule for the width of the bands is that they should be at least twice the width of the number of stitches required for the buttonhole, more if desired. Place the button on the stockinette stitch to count the number of necessary stitches. The buttonhole should not be in the center of the band. Allow one or two extra stitches toward the edge. For example, in an 8-stitch band using 4 stitches for the buttonhole, 3 stitches should be used at the outside edge, so when the cardigan is fastened, the button will not jut over the side.

BANDS

As the bands coming up the front only overlap once, it is necessary to add only half the required band stitches on each side, but knit a whole band of a special stitch, if you are not

48

using stockinette stitch, which should be strengthened with ribbon.

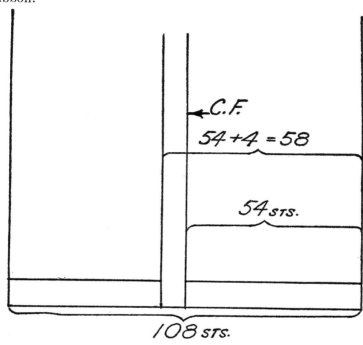

DIAGRAM 15.

Method

Follow diagram for front of cardigan.

In the example, there are 108 stitches across the back. ½ of 108 stitches is 54 to the center front. An 8-stitch band is being used; therefore, add half the width of the band, 4 stitches, which equals 58 stitches, 8 of these knitted in band-stitches, and 50 stitches in stockinette, or any texture stitch. This applies to both sides.

ZIPPERS

No extra stitches are added for zippers. Either single crochet the edges or use garter-stitch at the front opening for 3 or 4 stitches.

METHOD FOR FIGURING CARDIGAN FRONT

Half the total number of stitches required for the back, plus half the number of stitches necessary for the width of each band are the necessary number of stitches for each front.

POCKETS

The position of the pockets is important in any garment. There is a general rule which can be applied, whether breast, jacket, coat or pockets in sweaters, as far as the location from the seam to the center front is concerned.

    1. Figure the desired width of the pocket from the stitch gauge. An average woman's pocket is 4 inches wide, average man's is 5 inches.

    2. Subtract the necessary number of stitches for the pocket from the underarm to center-front stitches. See diagram 16.

    3. Divide the remaining stitches into ⅓, allowing ⅔ to the center-front and ⅓ toward the underarm seam.

The pocket is 5 inches wide and there are 6 stitches to the inch, 5 times 6 is 30 stitches for the pocket. 30 stitches from 54 stitches to the center front is 24 stitches. Dividing into ⅓, 16 stitches to the center front and 8 stitches to the underarm seam. See diagram.

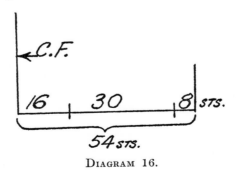

DIAGRAM 16.

Note: 1. The depth of a pocket should be equal to the width or longer.

2. The lower edge of the pocket in a cardigan should reach the top of the border.

3. Openings for breast pockets should be about 2 inches from the first bind-off at the armhole.

Method

1. Bind off the stitches for the pocket on the right side, the same as for a buttonhole. Knit a piece of stockinette stitch, using the same number of stitches as were bound off, and finish on a knit row. When purling back, use the stitches in the small piece to take the place of those that were bound off. This is the back of the pocket which is sewn down later.

2. Make a big buttonhole, then pick up the stitches afterward and knit down. This makes a firmer pocket.

PROJECTS

1. Diagram and chart the fronts of woman's and man's cardigan to armholes, placing the position of the pockets.

2. Diagram and chart your own sweater to the armholes.

3. Check the answers on pages 229 to 231.

CHAPTER 13

NECKLINES

THE NECKLINE of any garment is of the utmost importance and should be designed to be in harmony with the shape of the face and chin and the length of the throat. Also the general proportions of the body should be taken into consideration.

A tall, slender person, as a rule, has a long, thin neck, but this isn't always the case. A long pointed neckline exaggerates the length and thinness of the neck while it will modify the roundness in a full face. Also, shallow necklines with high, fitted up-at-the-back collars, as well as rolled collars, are good for a person with a long neck and also excellent to conceal a "dowager hump."

Shallow necklines, whether they are round, square or high oval, make the neck look shorter, but the contour of the face must also be considered. Chins must also come in for their share of attention. A square neckline should never be used with a square jaw because it repeats the same line, while a fairly deep oval will detract from the squareness. A pointed chin looks well in a high, round neckline but appears more pointed in a "V".

High, tight collars are generally trying to plump persons, just as collarless garments emphasize a long, thin neck, while flat collars that carry the line down are good for a short, thick neck.

A broad collar or lapels that carry the eye across the shoulders, make a person look broader, while a collar or lapels that carry the eye down toward the waist, have a tendency to make a person appear longer waisted, hence long lapels tend to slim the heavy figure.

For older persons, high necklines, or low ones that reveal the generally preserved skin of the upper chest, are good. Sagging, tell-tale chin wrinkles are often concealed by means of a scarf, ribbon with bow, or fastened with a brooch or pin.

HOW TO MEASURE THE POSITION OF THE NECKLINE

Having decided which is the most suitable neckline, it is necessary to know the lowest depth in front.

Method

1. Place the tape measure horizontally from armscye to armscye at the point where the shaping should be begun, remembering that if ribbing is going to be added for sweaters, one inch lower is necessary.
2. Now measure the distance from the tip of the shoulder. That means that if the neckline is to be started 4 inches below the tip of the shoulder (no matter what type) and half the armhole measurement is 10 inches, the neckline is begun when 6 inches of the armhole are knitted, measuring the curve.

1. *High, Round Neckline or Turtle Neck*
   (With an Opening)

A high, round neckline should reach the hollow of the throat, which is generally 2 inches below the tip of the shoulder in front for an adult and 1½ inches for a child. Follow diagram.

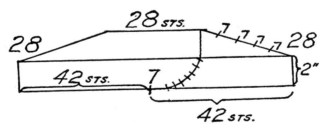

DIAGRAM 17.

Note: One third of the shoulder stitches to be used for the back of the neck.

Method

(a) Knit the armhole 2 inches shorter than the back, which is 8 inches.

(b) Knit across to half the total number of the shoulder-to-shoulder stitches—42, and place the remaining 42 stitches on a stitch holder or safety pin. Half the neckline is worked at one time.

(c) 42 stitches to the center front. 28 stitches required for the shoulder. 42 stitches minus 28 stitches equals 14 stitches to take off for half the neckline.

(d) The shaping of a round neckline is the same as the shaping of an armhole. Bind off half the total number of stitches at the beginning, then knit 2 together, every other row; that is, bind off 7 stitches at the neck edge, then knit 2 together, every other row, 7 times.

(e) Work the shoulder to correspond with the back shoulder.

(f) Complete the other side to correspond but reverse the shaping.

Note: If the armhole isn't the same length as the back knit even until the measurement is reached.

2. *Without an Opening—Slipover*

Follow Diagram 18.

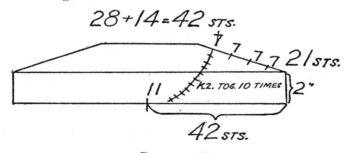

DIAGRAM 18.

The last step on both sides of the shoulder is not bound off, as explained in previous lesson. Therefore, there are 21 stitches for each shoulder and 28 plus 14 stitches for the back of the neck.

Method

(a) Work to the center of the total shoulder-to-shoulder stitches—84 stitches. This is 42 stitches. 42 stitches minus 21 stitches for the shoulder is 21 stitches for half the neckline. Using the same rule as above, half the stitches are bound off at the center front 11 stitches, then knit 2 together, 10 times, every other row.

Note: If the stitches are not completely decreased when the armhole measurement is reached, knit 2 together at the neck edge, at the same time as decreasing for the shoulders.

3. *Cardigan*

Note: All necklines except square necklines are figured from the center front. This is important when figuring for a cardigan. Follow diagram.

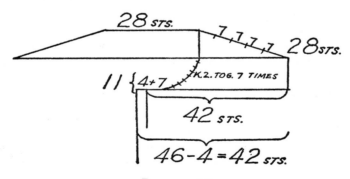

DIAGRAM 19.

Method

(a) The total of stitches for half the front after the armholes have been shaped, is 46 stitches minus half the

width of the band—4 stitches (to figure from the center front), is 42 stitches.

(b) 42 stitches minus 28 stitches for the shoulder equals 14 stitches, which is 7 stitches for the first bind-off and knit 2 together, 7 times.

(c) Half the width of the band is to be added to the first bind-off. 7 stitches plus 4 stitches is 11 stitches and knit 2 together, 7 times, on every front row.

METHODS FOR HIGH, ROUND NECKLINES

1. *High round neckline with opening—slipover*

   a. High, round necklines begin 2 inches below the tip of the shoulder for an adult, 1½ inches for a child.

   b. Knit to half the total shoulder to shoulder stitches, place the other half on a stitch holder.

   c. Subtract the shoulder stitches from the number of stitches to the center front.

   d. Shaping: same as for armhole. Bind off half the total number of stitches at the center front, then knit 2 together every front row, until the shoulder stitches remain.

   e. Work the shoulder to correspond with the back.

   f. Knit the other side to correspond, only in reverse.

2. *High round neck slipover—no opening*

   a. Don't work the last slope of each shoulder.

   b. Continue as above subtracting the adjusted shoulder measurement from half the total shoulder to shoulder measurement for the number of stitches to be decreased at the neck edge.

3. *Cardigan*

   Subtract half the width of the band first, then proceed as #1, adding half the band stitches to the first bind-off.

PROJECTS

1. On example of man's and woman's example sweaters, diagram and chart:
   a. High round neck slipover with opening.
   b. High round neck slipover without opening.
   c. High round neck for cardigan.
2. Check answers on pages 231 to 234.

HIGH ROUND NECK WITH MACHINE

Use 2 balls and shape the left side at the same time as the right, working in reverse.

CHAPTER 14

NECKLINES CONTINUED

"V" NECKLINES

"V" NECKLINES are centered the same way as round neck-lines, so work to the center front. The main thing to remember is that you decrease until the required number of stitches for the shoulder are left. How to decrease may be worked out exactly according to rows and the number of stitches to be decreased, but generally the following will suffice:

1. After the stitches have been bound off at the armhole or 2 inches from the first bind-off.

    Knit 2 together, every front row, that is every 2nd row, until the shoulder stitches remain. See diagram 20.

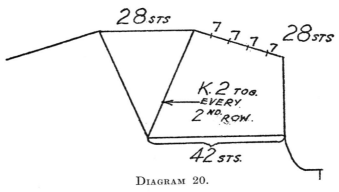

DIAGRAM 20.

2. At the first bind-off at the armhole.

    Knit 2 together, every 2nd front row, that is every 4th row, until the shoulder stitches remain.

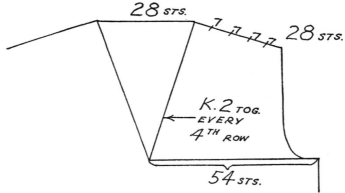

DIAGRAM 21.

3. Just above the waist line.

Knit 2 together every 8th row.

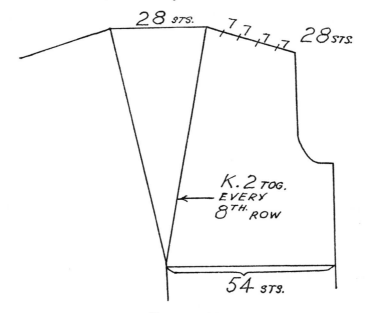

DIAGRAM 22.

Machine

Use 2 balls of yarn and work the left side at the same time as the right, in reverse.

"V" NECKLINES FOR CARDIGANS

1. The same decreases apply to cardigans, except that the decreases come inside the bands. However, it is better that the knit 2 together decrease is used for the left side and the decrease of slip, knit and pass, for the right.

2. Also, leave the number of stitches for the band, plus the stitches necessary for the shoulder, so the band stitches may be knitted around to the center back or a shoulder seam, where they may be joined.

SQUARE NECKLINES

Follow diagram 23. It is self-explanatory.

Bind off the center stitches and work the left front first, knitting straight to the tip of the shoulder, then shape the shoulder. Attach the yarn and work the right side to correspond, only in reverse.

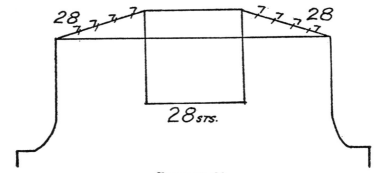

DIAGRAM 23.

PROJECTS

1. Diagram and chart "V" neckline for woman's example slipover sweater.
2. Diagram and chart own sweater to the shoulder.
3. Check answers on pages 235 and 236.

CHAPTER 15

SLEEVES

ALL SLEEVES SHOULD be comfortable and allow for freedom of movement. The type of sleeve depends upon the type of garment, the material used and, of course, the needs of the individual. Any sleeve, no matter how tight-fitting, should never be skin-tight.

There are many types of sleeves, long, short, three-quarters, dolman, etc., with caps that fit into the armhole with no extra fullness and some that are slightly gathered. Also they can be of many and varied widths according to the dictates of fashion.

In sewing today, there is only a slight difference in the right and left sleeve, while in knitting both the right and left sleeves are the same.

LONG SLEEVES
(We shall figure the example first.)

Measurements

Wrist	6 inches
Upperarm	11 inches
Sleeve Underarm Length	18 inches

Stitch Gauge—6 stitches to the inch

Follow diagram 24.

Method

1. 6 inches plus 1 inch at the wrist, times 6 stitches to the inch, is 42 stitches. 44 stitches for K. 2, P. 2, the same as the ribbing at the bottom of the sweater. Knit 2 inches of ribbing or more.

2. At least 1 inch of stitches is added on the first row after the ribbing, 6 stitches. 44 stitches plus 6 stitches = 50

61

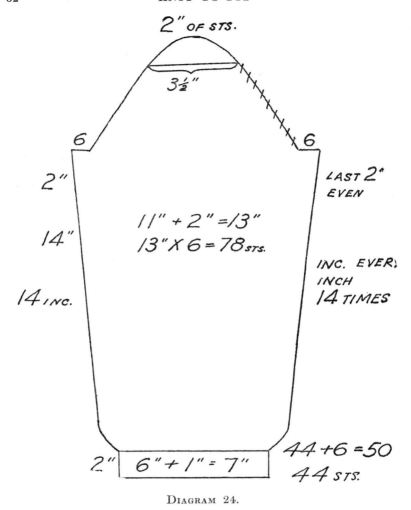

DIAGRAM 24.

stitches. 6 into 44 goes 7 times, so increase in every 7th stitch.

3. The upperarm measurement is 11 inches plus 2 inches = 13 inches. 13 times 6 stitches to the inch = 78 stitches. 50 stitches from 78 stitches is 28 stitches. 14 stitches to

increase on each side. (Increases should be completed from 2 to 4 inches from the underarm.)

4. The underarm measurement is 18 inches, so increase at both sides every inch, 14 times, then knit 2 inches even, or until the underarm measures 18 inches.

5. *Cap or top of sleeve*

Bind off 6 stitches to match the underarms at the beginning of the next 2 rows, then knit 2 together at the beginning and the end of the knitted rows (front), until 3½ inches of stitches remain, 22 stitches. Now bind off 2 stitches at the beginning of every row until 2 inches of stitches are left, 12 stitches. Bind off. Around the cap of the sleeve will be the armhole measurement.

Note: 1. When measuring for a child's upperarm, take an exact measurement, the same as for an adult, then add at least 1½ inches to the upperarm measurement. An extra long cuff may be knitted to add length.

2. A man doesn't like a tight sleeve. Begin with 2 inches more at the wrist and add 2 inches of stitches after the ribbing, also allow 3 inches more than the actual upperarm measurement.

METHOD FOR LONG SLEEVES

1. The wrist measurement plus one inch, times the stitch gauge provide the least number of stitches for the cuff. Wider if desired.

2. Add one inch of stitches or more on the first row after the ribbing.

3. Add 2 inches or more for a woman, 3 inches for a man, and 1½ inches for a child, to the upperarm measurement.

4. The difference between the stitches above the cuff or rib and the stitches required at the upperarm, equals the number of stitches to be added on both sides—½ at each.

5. Divide the number of stitches to be increased at one side into the length of sleeve above the cuff to know where to increase—allow 2 to 4 inches even.

Cap

6. Bind off the same number of stitches as the back and front underarms, then knit 2 together at the beginning and end of every other row, until 3½ inches of stitches remain, then bind off 2 stitches at the beginning of every row, until 2 inches of stitches are left. Bind off all the stitches.

Note: 1. When sleeves are wider than the necessary increase at the upperarm, when knitting the cap, the surplus width must be reduced. Generally, at 3½ inches of stitches, we bind off 2 stitches at the beginning of the rows but for every extra inch added, begin to bind off 2 stitches one inch sooner. For example, at 4½ inches, 5½ inches, etc.

2. The depth of a woman's cap is 5½ inches or more, a man's is 6½ inches or more and a child's is 3 inches.

3. Half the curve around the cap should be the same as half the armhole measurement.

PROJECTS

1. Diagram and chart the man's and woman's long sleeves of the example sweaters, using 6 stitches to the inch for the man, and 7 stitches to the inch for the woman.
2. Diagram and chart your own sweater sleeve.

Check answers on pages 236 to 238.

CHAPTER 16

SHORT SLEEVES

SHORT SLEEVES may be many lengths and widths depending upon the type of material, individual needs, and the purpose of the garment. They may also be knitted with or without ribbing or bands.

A short, straight sleeve, like a long sleeve, must have at least 2 inches added to the upperarm measurement for width, and may vary from 2 inches to $5\frac{1}{2}$ inches in length. The cap is finished the same as for a long sleeve. See diagram 25.

A short, action sleeve is more generous in width, 3 or 4 inches more than the upperarm measurement, yet not too wide for good styling and without a cuff. These are shaped at the underarm seam and so too much fullness isn't taken out at the seam; the sleeve is begun with more width.

As for long sleeves, the cap should fit into the armhole so if 3 inches of stitches are added for a woman, at the upperarm, at $4\frac{1}{2}$ inches of stitches, bind off 2 stitches at the beginning of every row, until 2 inches of stitches remain, then bind off.

TO START FROM THE TOP

Sometimes it is advisable to start a sleeve at the top.

Method

Diagram and chart as though beginning at the bottom. Cast on 2 inches of stitches, then add 2 stitches at the beginning of every row until you have $3\frac{1}{2}$ inches of stitches. Now increase a stitch at the beginning and end of every row (front) until the cap is the same size as the armhole. Then add the same number of stitches at each end that were bound off at the back and front underarms. Continue knitting the sleeve, in reverse.

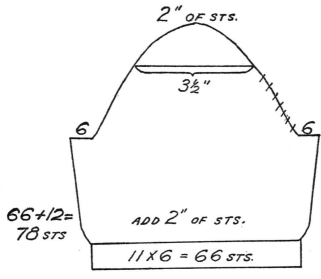

DIAGRAM 25.

METHOD FOR SHORT SLEEVES

1. Use the upperarm measurement for a narrow ribbing.
2. Add at least 2 inches of stitches on the first row after the ribbing, more if desired.
3. Complete the cap, the same as for long sleeve.

PROJECT

1. Diagram and chart a short sleeve, 5 inches long and 3 inches wider than the upperarm measurement for your woman's example sweater. Stitch gauge is 7 sts. to the inch.
2. Check your answers on page 240.

Note: For a woman with large upperarms, ¾ sleeves are good. It may be a straight sleeve, having the necessary width at the upperarm, or may nearly fit around the forearm and the stitches may be added immediately after the ribbing, or quickly at the sides.

CHAPTER 17

COMPLETION OF SWEATERS

TODAY WE CONSIDER knitting and crocheting in the same light as sewing. Each piece is shaped separately according to the necessary measurements, sleeves are made the suitable width and length and the caps are deep enough so that neither the shoulder nor the neckline is pulled out of shape. Now the sweater has to be completed, so that we have a finished, custom-made look.

As in sewing, the ribbing at the neck, collars, etc., are completed after the larger pieces are fastened together, with the exception of a slipover sweater without an opening—the ribbing at the front is knitted first.

The seams used to be either woven or overcast together on the wrong side, which is all right for baby sweaters and very fine yarn, but a much better way is to slip stitch (crochet) the pieces together on the wrong side. A #5 steel crochet hook is adequate for nearly all types of materials. Never use a bone hook as it makes the stitches too loose.

A SLIP STITCH IN CROCHET

Method

Place the two seams together, wrong side out, and insert the hook through the two folds not quite ⅛ of an inch deep. Place the thread over the hook and draw the thread through the folds and the loop on the hook.

Split the yarn if it is too heavy.

Note: 1. Be sure the seams are as elastic as the rest of the garment but they shouldn't show on the right side.

2. Join the underarm seams, sleeve seams, then shoulders.

67

When putting the shoulders together, slip-stitch deeper at the beginning of each slope.

3. Pin in the sleeves at the armholes, with the seam at the underarm seam, and the center of the top of the cap at the shoulder seam. Slip-stitch in place.

THE NUMBER OF STITCHES TO PICK UP AROUND THE NECK

Become accustomed to using your tape measure. For slip-over, round necklines, measure from the shoulder seam to the center front. If this is $5\frac{1}{2}$ inches and there are 6 stitches to the inch, use an even number of stitches for each side—68 stitches from shoulder to shoulder seam. For the back of the neck, the same number of stitches are used as were bound off.

Note: 1. Pick up the stitches around a neckline or armhole for ribbing, or the completion of a pocket, on the right side. For collars, measure the length as above, but pick up the stitches on the wrong side.

2. If smaller needles are used for picking up the stitches around a neckline the gauge of the smaller needles must be used.

Method

Place the point of the needle into a stitch, then pass the yarn around the needle as if to knit and draw the loop through to make a stitch. Be sure to put the needle in deep enough so no holes are formed. Picked up stitches should look like a continuation of the fabric.

PICKING UP STITCHES NEAR KNIT 2 TOGETHER DECREASES

Picking up stitches near knit 2 together decreases can sometimes be a problem. It is better not to pick up the loose stitch between the two decreases (for this causes a hole) but rather to pick up a stitch immediately below the actual decrease, then one in the decrease itself.

Knit the knits and *purl the purls* when binding off. The ribbing is generally one-inch wide, six to eight inches, for a turtle neck.

MITER FOR A "V" NECK

Mark the center of the "V" with a safety pin. Measure the inches, hence the stitches to the center front, as for a round neckline. Allow 2 knit stitches right in the center of the "V" and 4 purl stitches on each side. This is done by counting from the center after all the stitches have been picked up, so coming back on the wrong side, it will be K. 4, P. 2, K. 4, in the center.

Decrease on the 4 purl stitches, on both sides of the K. 2, every front row, until P. 1 remains. If necessary, K. 2 together in the center.

RIBBON DOWN THE FRONT

If ribbon is going to be sewn down the front, it is better to do this after the sweater has been steamed, then the correct length of the ribbon can be ascertained. I suggest measuring the length when the sweater is worn. Allow one extra inch of ribbon for turn-unders. Baste and overcast the ribbon. Baste the button-holes and the ribbon together. Cut the buttonholes in the ribbon, then buttonhole stitch on both the sweater and the ribbon at the same time.

COLLARS

Round Flat Collar for a High Round Neckline

Method

1. Measure the inches from the center front to the shoulder seam and multiply by the stitch gauge.
2. Pick up the stitches, on the wrong side, from the center front to the shoulder seam, continue around the back, picking up the same number of stitches as were bound off, then pick up the stitches on the other half front.
3. Purl a row, knit a row, purl a row, and on the 4th row, increase before and after the shoulder seams. This makes 4 increases.
4. Continue to increase every 4th row, about one inch from each shoulder seam, until the desired depth of collar.
5. Single crochet twice around the collar to make it lie flat.

ILLUSTRATION 12.

STAND-UP COLLAR (at the back)

Method

1. Pick up the stitches the same as for a round collar and knit even in stockinette stitch or ribbing, as desired, for $3\frac{1}{2}$ or 4 inches. If points are desired at the front, increase at the beginning and end of every 4th row.

Note: If stockinette stitch is used, single crochet on the right side twice, tightly.

LAPELS

1. The easiest lapels to make are those where the neckline isn't bound off [as in the illustration] and the garment is knitted straight at the center front. The shoulders are shaped when the armhole measurement is reached, then the remaining stitches are bound off loosely. This, of course, gives the wrong side of the material when the lapel is turned to the front; but if the remainder of the stitches for the collar are knitted on the wrong side, this is permissible.
2. Decrease the same as for a "V" neckline and knit separate pieces for lapels, starting with 4 stitches and increasing where you decreased on the garment.

Note: 1. If wider lapel is desired, increase at the outer edge.
2. The dart stitches in a jacket may be used to widen a lapel.

ADDING COLLAR [NOTCHED]

Method

1. Pick up the stitches on the right side of the lapel (about 2 inches from the shoulder seam depending upon the width) around the back of the neck, then the other lapel and work for $3\frac{1}{2}$ inches. Bind off loosely and crochet around the lapels and collar, twice on the right side to make them stay flat.

ROLLED COLLARS

Note: A "V" neckline which may be either deep or shallow is necessary.

Method

All the stitches are picked up at one time, on the wrong side (See Round Collar). Work 6 rows even, then bind off half an inch of stitches at the beginning of every row, until the desired width of the collar. Bind off all the stitches loosely. Single crochet twice to keep the collar flat.

PROJECT

1. Make a small "V" neckline and miter the "V".
2. Complete your own sweater.

CHAPTER 18

BLOCKING A SWEATER

ACTUALLY, a sweater knitted from correct measurements shouldn't have to be blocked. It should just be steamed flat. A steam iron is excellent for this. Have you tried the sweater on to see how the shoulders fit? Did you tighten the armscye when putting in the sleeve? Are all your seams elastic? Does it feel comfortable? Are your stitches picked up neatly? Are you satisfied with the result? Can you diagram and chart any type of Slip-over or Cardigan (not fitted) using any material and for any person? You should be able to since that was the purpose of the previous chapters and from now on, we shall apply the techniques of shaping, to other garments.

BLOCKING

In the first place, I definitely do not agree with blocking any garment made of wool or partly wool-yarn, in separate pieces. The elasticity of the yarn allows the pieces to be stretched and I have seen some sad shapes, when supposedly blocked in pieces, by someone who did not understand what they were doing.

Ribbon knits are a different matter; we shall discuss these later in the course.

MATERIALS REQUIRED FOR BLOCKING

1. A large table
2. A heavy pad for a base to which the garment may be pinned.
3. Cloth to cover pad—unbleached muslin is satisfactory.

4. A long wooden rule.
5. Non-rusting blocking pins.
6. Steam or electric iron.
7. Cloths for steaming which should be neither too thick nor too thin. Used Turkish towels are good.
8. A sleeve pressing board.

Method

1. Turn garment inside out.
2. With pins, mark the center back of sweater.
3. On blocking board place pins at "A" and "B", where center back is to be pinned. Pin the center back to the board.
4. With the rule, mark a line "CD", where waist is pinned, using half the waist measurement, one-quarter on each side of "AB".

Note: The center back and sides are pinned, before the fronts are pinned down in a Cardigan.

5. At "D" measure "DF" which is the underarm to waist measurement.
6. Measure "EF" which is half the bust measurement, one-quarter on each side of "AB".
7. Pin the sweater to measurements and check.
8. Spread the armscyes until the correct measurement is obtained. Pin to board.
9. Test the shoulders to see if correct width—adjust width by means of armscyes, then pin to board, being sure that both sides are equal distances from the center.
10. If Cardigan, pin down the center fronts, allowing for overlap.
11. Adjust neckline and pin in position.
12. Measure the sleeve underarm length and pin the sleeves in position, "EK" and "FJ".
13. Check width of the sleeves and pin.

Note: Never steam ribbing since it should not be stretched.

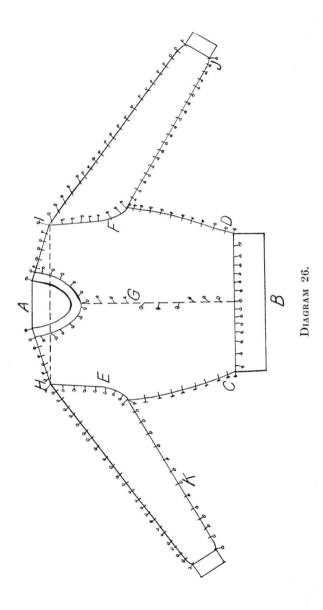

DIAGRAM 26.

14. Dampen cloth in warm water and place it over the garment.
15. Steam with a hot iron but be sure to keep weight of iron in the *hand*. If weight is allowed to press down wool, it will leave a shiny mark and shrink it.

Note: Steam iron may be used instead of cloth if there is definitely no stretching required.

16. Leave on the pad until dry.
17. Take out the pins; steam the seams using sleeve board where necessary. Be sure to remove the pin marks.

Note: If garment is made to fit, place pins one inch apart— more may be needed if tight.

PROJECT

Test your blocking ability on any sweater.

CHAPTER 19

COLOR

TODAY NEARLY every woman knows the value of charm, so we must be on the alert to find an irresistible color when we are considering any form of dress design.

I want to stress that one should never choose a color because it happens to be in vogue for that particular season. Too, one must remember that as we grow older, the pigmentation of skin, eyes and hair change. Also, those with tinted hair must be careful. Subdued colors are essential especially close to the face, so as not to call attention to the inevitable lines.

It is a good idea to have a range of your own colors—pieces of material large enough to drape around the upper part of the bust and throat, and of different textures, if possible. Texture can alter the effect that a color produces. A vivid color may look harsh in a hard-surfaced fabric, but if the fabric has depth, it may become vibrant and flattering. Choose a piece of material comparable to the material you wish to use, depending upon the purpose, the occasion, the season, and if one is traveling.

One of the important things neglected in many knit shops is the importance of color. Prestige would be gained if more emphasis were placed on it. To keep a customer, one must be completely satisfied after the garment is tried and tested. But be sure you have sufficient quantity of material of that particular color in stock. Having to wait two or three weeks for material would dampen the ardor of any woman.

Industry has taken advantage of the vast new potential of color. Exciting, uncommon colors have been created by the yarn manufacturers.

COLORS

Red

Red is exhilarating. Recently, it has blossomed forth in all its glory, alone or with a combination of color; and, it is fashionable for any season of the year. However, if one is traveling, it is well to remember that red is taboo in some countries of Europe as well as the British Isles during the summer. It is rich, warm and aggressive and really more suitable for cooler seasons. Also, older women with good figures may look well in some shades of red, but should be wary of having it too bright a color or too close to the face. Something soft in material and subdued in color would be more pleasing. Try adding a chiffon scarf of pink. Shades of pink have an air of festivity and the right shade can be worn by almost anyone.

Blue

Blue gives a sense of relaxation. There are cool and serene grayed-blues, and warm and exotic ones, but pick the tones that *accentuate* rather than *diminish* your own coloring. Some blues may be so strong that they detract from the color of your eyes, and make them appear wishy-washy.

Green

Green may be refreshing and cool, but beware of yellow-green if your complexion is sallow.

Yellow

Yellow with its many shades from yellow-beige to orange is used a great deal and can give a sense of well-being.

Gray is neutral, while *purple* is dramatic.

Black and *white* are in a category apart. Those with fading color and graying hair should remember that black absorbs light and tends to drain color from the face. *White* reflects heat and so is considered the coolest color.

IMPORTANCE OF COLOR WITH RESPECT TO FIGURE PROBLEMS

Is the color suitable for your figure proportions? Should you wear one solid color or should some subtle trickery be used to hide some figure discrepancies?

Black or grayed colors tend to make the figure appear smaller and slimmer than do bright and light colors.

A bright panel from neck to hem makes the wearer look taller.

One who wishes to appear shorter may use a two-tone effect, broken across the figure.

To minimize the waist, use a band of cool color or change the width of the belt.

A large bust can be minimized by the use of diagonal lines or by wearing dark or cool colors on top portion of garment, and bright colors at the bottom.

PROJECT

Since choosing the correct colors is a very important phase of knit design, study colored fashion illustrations from magazines and books, and consider why they attract you. Notice what colors are chosen for a particular type of person and the style of the garment.

SELECTING COLORS TO SUIT
INDIVIDUAL NEEDS

COMPLEXION—hair and eye colors are so interrelated that they must all be considered when selecting colors.

SKIN OR COMPLEXION

Does the color make you look more pale, more sallow or rosier? This is an important question. It must be understood that the lower the natural pigmentation, the softer, less-accented the color should be. All skins are white, yellow or pink in varying degrees. If yellow is the predominating hue the skin is considered warm-toned, so wear colors that blend with yellow, shades from red-orange to yellow, red-browns, rose-beiges and golden-yellows. When pink predominates, the skin is pink-toned and cool in appearance and therefore needs no highlighting, so soft muted colors should be worn.

Hair

White hair is the coolest. Black comes next because it hasn't any warmth. The third in coolness is light ash-blond. Golden blonds are definitely warm, while redheads, ranging from light golden-red to auburn, are in the warm category.

Eyes

Eyes are classified as warm or cool also. The brown group are considered warm, hazel eyes warm-to-cool [according to whether the brown flecks predominate], and all the blues and grays are cool.

Light and True Blonds

This is applied to those whose complexion ranges from very fair to golden tones, hair light, to golden blond, and eyes may be light blue to brown. This person may wear colors that are clear and fresh looking, blues, purples, greens, and any pastels. Black too may be very stunning. However, if the coloring is very delicate be sure it isn't overpowered with vivid colors. Emphasize this delicacy; it is an asset.

Medium Blonds

Usually a medium blond has a medium complexion, hair between blond and light brown, and eyes that run the gamut from blue to brown—the same categories as the light blonds, but not as vivid since they would detract from the neutral, natural coloring of the hair and skin.

Auburn

The person with true red or auburn may have a very fair skin or it may be as dark as a brunette's, with blue, gray, hazel or dark brown eyes. Blues, greens and attractive browns are good. Reds, pinks, deep purples are taboo. But whether white or yellow predominates in the skin tones, the auburn-haired has distinctive coloring that should be made the most of.

Similarly, a brunette of the "Irish type," white skin, blue or blue-gray eyes and dark hair is extremely attractive because of the striking contrast.

Medium Brunette

A medium brunette may have hair which is chestnut or brown, eyes blue to brown, and skin fair to olive. As this is the most predominant "type" in America, one needs to pay special attention to details that raise her out of the general run. She should use very distinctive colors definitely not drab, adding a touch of exotic to her appearance.

Dark Brunette

Her skin may be very fair to olive, hair brown to black, and eyes varying from blue-gray to black. She may wear true colors in most instances, but if she has a sallow complexion, too yellow-greens or orange will emphasize her sallow skin.

Gray-haired

Sometimes when natural pigmentation leaves the skin, it may develop a clear almost cameo quality. Soft and subtle colors and white emphasize this ethereal look. If your hair is steel-gray or pure white, with few exceptions, you may follow the dictates of your eyes and skin colors. But if your hair is streaked with yellowish or brownish wisps, be careful not to emphasize these. Avoid yellow, brown and tan. And above all, one should dress according to one's age.

PROJECT

Read articles on color, charm and personality. Have files for *Light Blonds, Medium Blonds, Medium Brunette, Dark Brunette,* and *Gray.*

CHAPTER 21

SLEEVELESS SWEATERS, WESKITS
AND JERKINS

GENERALLY speaking, sleeveless sweaters are badly designed in knitting. I have seen movie stars in advertisements wearing sleeveless sweaters that were very poorly styled, having tight armholes and shoulders which were too long. They should allow for freedom of movement, that means there should be no constriction at the armhole or the neckline.

There are 5 main differences between diagramming and charting a sleeveless sweater from one with set-in sleeves.

1. The underarm to waist measurement is one inch shorter.

2. Half the armhole measurement is one inch longer, to make up for the one inch deducted from the underarm to waist measurement.

3. The shoulder-to-shoulder measurement is one inch shorter on each side, which means two inches altogether.

4. The one inch deducted from the shoulders is added to the first bind-off, at the armhole.

5. Allow one fewer slope at the shoulders according to the stitch gauge.

See diagrams 27 and 28, using measurements from Chapter 5—page 19. They are self-explanatory.

Note: 1. Always diagram and chart the body of a sweater with set-in sleeves first.

2. The stitches around the armhole are picked up after the body of the sweater is completed. This is one inch wide, making the full shoulder-to-shoulder measurement.

3. The neckline is finished the same as for a sweater with set-in sleeves.

83

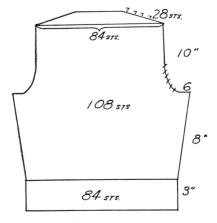

7 7 7 28 STS.
84 STS.
10"
6
108 STS
8"
84 STS.
3"

DIAGRAM 27.

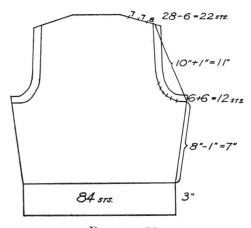

7 7 8   28−6 =22 STS.
10"+1"=11"
6+6 =12 STS.
8"−1"=7"
84 STS.
3"

DIAGRAM 28.

POSITION OF CABLES

Turn to *Chapter 11* for the rule concerning cables.

Method

1. 2 extra stitches are added for each cable, which means that 10 extra stitches must be added for 5 cables, and so on.

2. Using figures from diagram 27, and adding 5 cables to the body of the sweater of P. 2, K. 6, P. 2, that is, 108 stitches plus 10 stitches, which makes 118 stitches.

3. Each cable requires 10 stitches, so 5 cables equals 5 times 10, which is 50 stitches.

4. 50 stitches from 118 stitches, leaves 68 stitches for 6 spaces.

5. 6 into 68 goes 11 times and 2 over, so knit 11 stitches between each cable, except at the ends where you have to knit 12 stitches. See diagram 29.

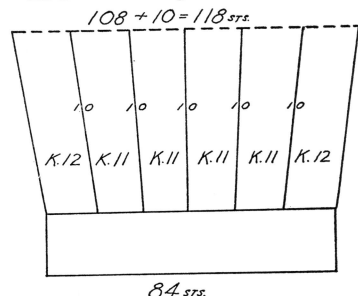

DIAGRAM 29.

Note: 1. Always diagram without the cables first, then add the extra stitches for the body of the sweater. This means that the figuring will be the same as for a sweater without cables, except for the figuring of the first cable row.

2. For the shaping at the armhole, neck and shoulders, knit 2 together twice at each cable to eliminate the extra stitches.

3. It isn't necessary to have cables both at the back and front of a sweater. Cables often are placed at the front and one or two for the sleeves.

PROJECT

1. On the sample measurements of *Chapter 6* on page 24, diagram and chart the backs of sleeveless sweaters for both a man and woman.
2. On the man's measurements of *Chapter 6*, diagram the front of a cable sweater to the armhole, having 5 cables of P. 2, K. 6, P. 2, evenly spaced.
3. Check answers on pages 241 to 245.

CHAPTER 22

FITTED WESKITS AND JERKINS

FITTED weskits and jerkins are diagrammed and charted the
same as sleeveless sweaters except for the increases for the bust,
which are gradually added at the sides.

Method

We shall use for our example the same measurements as in
Chapter 5. If this had been a weskit, the 84 stitches for the
waist (back) would be subtracted from across the 108 back
underarm stitches, which leaves 24 stitches. See diagram 30.
There are 7 inches to the underarm, therefore, if one stitch is
increased on both sides, every ½ inch, 12 times, and the last
1 inch knitted even, there will be 108 stitches.

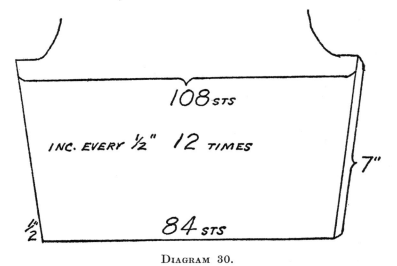

DIAGRAM 30.
87

METHOD FOR INCREASING AT THE SIDES

1. Half the waist measurement subtracted from half the bust measurement equals the number of stitches to add at the underarm seams.

2. Divide by 2 to find the number of stitches to add at each side.

3. Divide the number of stitches to increase into the inches at the underarm seam, to know where to increase.

Note: As the fullest part of the bust comes from two to four inches below the armpit, it is better to complete all the increases before that point.

BANDS

While weskits and jerkins do not have actual bands down the front, extra stitches must be allowed, the same as for a cardigan and the position of the buttons marked first.

As a weskit is a tight-fitting garment, many buttonholes are required; one inch to one-and-a-half inches apart is satisfactory. Be sure the top buttonhole will be in the correct position before starting any of the buttonholes.

POCKETS

The position of the pockets is exactly the same for weskits as for any other garment.

FRONTS

Left Front
Method

Charting the front without any points and allowing 4 extra stitches on both sides for buttons and buttonholes, there would be half of the 84 stitches, 42 stitches plus 4 stitches = 46 stitches at the waist.

Increase at the underarm seam, the same as the back, making the last inch even.

POINTS AT THE FRONT

The points come toward the center front, allowing one-third of the number of stitches and two-thirds towards the underarm seam. They are from three to three-and-a-half inches in depth, with the greatest slope towards the front. One-third of 42 stitches is 14 stitches and two-thirds is 28 stitches. Start the left front first with 2 stitches and increase 1 stitch toward the center front and 2 toward the underarm seam, every other row, until 42 stitches are made, adding the last 4 stitches all at one time, for the overlap at the front, making 46 stitches, the desired number. See diagram 31.

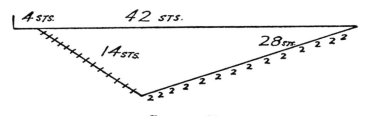

DIAGRAM 31.

PROJECT

1. Diagram and chart a weskit left front, with a square neckline on the woman's sample measurements in *Chapter 6*.
2. Check the answer on pages 245 and 246.

CHAPTER 23

FITTED SWEATERS

IT IS WELL to remember that only a person with a good figure and perfect carriage should wear tight-fitting garments; this applies especially to fitted sweaters, and even then, one must always allow sufficient room for freedom of movement. With the advent of scientifically designed girdles and bras, more women have supposedly good figures than previously.

I do not want you, however, to get a wrong impression about knits. Remember, I said, "tight-fitting garments." Any woman may wear knits, if they are correctly styled. That is why, throughout the entire course, I have stressed the correct method of measurements and individual design.

In the previous chapter we considered weskits fitted at the underarm seam.

One more measurement is required for a fitted sweater than for a weskit, if it starts below the waist. Again, we must be careful that the length suits individual needs.

At the desired depth, take the measurement around the body. Care must be taken that the tape doesn't drop either at the front or back and it must be loose enough so the flat of the hand may pass under the tape.

Method

In the previous lesson, we considered fitted weskits. The same principle applies to fitted sweaters. However, we use the underarm to waist and armhole measurements, as for a sweater with set-in sleeves. See diagram 32.

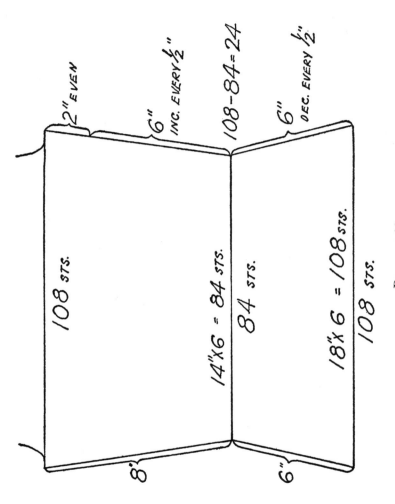

2" EVEN

6"
INC. EVERY ½"

108 – 84 = 24

6"
DEC. EVERY ½"

108 STS.

14"×6 = 84 STS.

84 STS.

18"×6 = 108 STS.

108 STS.

8"

6"

DIAGRAM 32.

Measurements

Waist .... 28 inches
Bust .... 36 inches
Waist to underarm .... 8 inches
Armhole .... 18 inches
Hip (6 inches below the waist) ... 36 inches
Stitch Gauge—6 stitches to the inch.

Study diagram 32. It is self-explanatory.

Note: Generally, the fronts and backs of tight-fitting sweaters are the same width. For sweaters for the evening it may be necessary to allow more width at the front. We discuss this later.

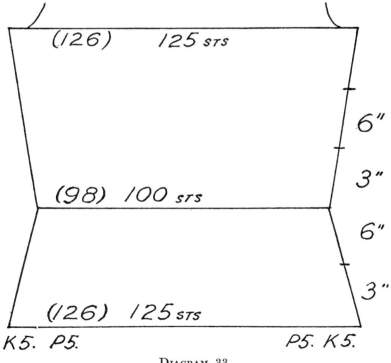

DIAGRAM 33.

RIBBED FITTED SWEATERS

Ribbed, fitted sweaters are decreased and increased in the same manner. However, if the ribs are large and there are too many increases and decreases to be made at the sides, it is advisable to have the increases and decreases in the ribs at even intervals. See diagram 33.

It should be understood that both sides of a ribbed garment should be the same, so if we begin with K. 5 of a K. 5, P. 5 rib, we should end with K. 5, therefore, the number should be divisible by 10 plus 5.

The same measurements as previously are used. There are 25 stitches to decrease to the waist in 13 knitted ribs and 12 purled ribs. Knit 3 inches even, then decrease in the knit ribs, 13 stitches, and 3 more inches and decrease in the purl ribs, 12 stitches. Increase in a similar manner, ending with 2 inches even.

PROJECT

1. Using the measurements and stitch gauge of the woman's sweater in *Chapter 6* and considering the measurement around the hip 36 inches, 6 inches below the waist, diagram the front of a fitted sweater with oval neckline, starting 4 inches below the tip of the shoulder.
2. Check answers on pages 247 and 248.

SWEATERS AND BLOUSES USING LACE STITCHES

IN ALL GARMENTS, the type of stitch that should be used is very important. A lace stitch for a tight-fitting garment is taboo. The beauty of lace, no matter how a garment is designed, lies in its delicate beauty and soft folds. However, the portion below the waist on a sweater or blouse may be fitted and knitted in stockinette stitch, then the increasing for the lace added at the waist, the same as for basic sweaters. Take the stitch gauge from a sample of the lace stitch which has been steamed, but not stretched.

Note: Be sure you know the lace pattern before starting any garment. You will save hours of time and discouragement.

In the Paris hand-knit collections, very fine yarn, dexterously knitted into lace blouses, dresses, etc., are evident. Of course, this type of work entails a great deal of very careful knitting. They are exquisite for tea, cocktails or evening occasions, although if one has a knit shop or gives instructions, it is advisable to steer clear of intricate lace patterns. In the first place, it is from the sale of materials that one's livelihood depends, and fine yarn, where little weight is used, means less material. Secondly, shaping with lace patterns is often difficult for the layman.

NECKLINES IN LACE SWEATERS AND BLOUSES

When using lace patterns, it is advisable to have a stockinette stitch yoke, then no difficulty is encountered when shaping. However, if lace is desired right up to the neckline, a square one is the simplest, so use this type if possible. If a round neckline is desired, follow the same directions as for the armhole shaping, which follow:

Allow one or more whole patterns for the shaping. For example, if there are 12 whole patterns for across the back, and there are 8 whole patterns for the shoulder, that means that 2 patterns are to be taken off for each armhole. After binding off one whole pattern, place a marker after the second pattern, and keep these stitches using stockinette stitch until all the stitches have been decreased.

LACE PATTERNS FOR HAND KNITTING

#1.

A multiple of 6 stitches plus 1. YO means Yarn Over.

Row 1: * K. 1, K. 2 tog., YO, K. 1, YO, K. 2 tog., repeat from * ending K. 1.

Row 2: Purl.

Rows 3 to 6: Repeat Rows 1 and 2, twice.

Row 7: Knit.

Row 8: Purl.

Repeat the 8 rows.

Alternate the pattern by starting with K. 3, then continue as above.

ILLUSTRATION 13.

#2.

A multiple of 8 stitches plus 1.

Row 1: K. 3, * YO, Sl 1, K. 2 tog., Pass sl st over K, YO, K. 5, repeat from * across the row, ending YO, Sl 1, K. 2 tog., Pass, YO, K. 3.

Row 2 and all even rows: Purl.

Row 3: K. 2 tog., K. 1, * YO, K. 3, YO, K. 1, Sl 1, K. 2 tog., Pass, K. 1, repeat from * across, ending YO, K. 3, YO, K. 1, K. 2 tog.

Row 5: K. 2 tog., * YO, K. 5, YO, Sl 1, K. 2 tog., Pass, repeat from * across, ending YO, K. 5, YO, K. 2 tog.

Row 7: K. 2, * YO, K. 1, Sl 1, K. 2 tog., Pass, K. 1, YO, K. 3, repeat from * across, ending K. 2 instead of K. 3.

Row 8: Purl.

Repeat rows 1 to 8.

ILLUSTRATION 14.

LACE PATTERNS ON MACHINE

As lace patterns require much moving of stitches on a machine, always try to use a simple pattern that will look well with the least amount of changing the position of stitches.

In machine knitting, as in hand-knitting, yarn overs are the basis for all lace patterns along with knit 2 togethers to make up for the extra stitch that was added.

Two stitches are placed on one needle, either to the right or left, and the empty needle left in working position to take the place of the yarn over. Then on the next row, all the stitches are worked, creating a hole. Bearing this in mind, a lace pattern intended for hand-knitting, may be worked on a machine. See illustration 13.

#1.

(a) Transfer the stitches 4, 10, 16, etc., onto needles 3, 9, 15, etc., stitches 6, 12, 18 onto needles 7, 13, 19 (same as knit 2 together).

(b) Keep the empty needles in working position and knit across twice.

(c) Repeat a and b twice more.

(d) Knit 5 rows then alternate the pattern, as in illustration.

#2.

(a) Transfer every 8th stitch to the next needle at the left.

(b) Knit across twice.

(c) Counting from the left, transfer stitches 9, 17, 25, etc., to their adjacent needles at the right, and 7, 15, 23, etc., to their next needles at the left.

ILLUSTRATION 15.

(d) Knit across twice.

(e) Transfer stitches 10, 18, 26, etc., to their next needles at the right, and stitches 6, 14, 22, etc., to their next needles at the left.

(f) Knit across twice.

(g) Transfer stitches 11, 19, 27, etc., to their adjacent needles at the right, and stitches 5, 13, 21, etc., to their adjacent needles to the left.

(h) Knit across twice.

(i) Repeat steps a to h, alternating the pattern as in illustration 15.

CHAPTER **25**

EVENING SWEATERS

SHEER GLAMOR for evening! Evening sweaters are sophisti-
cated for after dark in America—bare-shouldered, scoop necklines, with or without slender, tapering sleeves, cap sleeves or
no sleeves, made of very fine wool or linen yarn intermingled
with metallic thread and contrasted with short or full-length
skirts of glinting silk, mousseline, or layers of softly shaded
tulle or organdy or the swish of taffeta. Too, one might desire
a knitted skirt of soft, dainty yarn and metallic thread which
resembles lamé.

If you have understood the instructions so far, it shouldn't
be difficult to transform the knowledge, with added suggestions,
to evening sweaters.

NECKLINES

First we shall consider lower necklines.

As we learned in our earlier lessons on necklines (re-read
Chapters 13 and *14*) they are extremely important in dress
design. Strange as it may seem, low necklines are flattering for
older women, especially those who take care of their carriage
and have no "dowager hump." The wrinkles around the throat
line may be concealed by means of ropes of beads, ribbon with
flowers spilling from the throat, or a small knitted scarf, etc.

Instructions for all necklines—position

Having decided the type of neckline for both the front and
back, with tape measure held horizontally across from armscye
to armscye, the depth of the center front of the neckline to-be,
measure the distance from the tip of the shoulder, also the
depth of the neckline at the armscye.

99

Follow diagram 34. This is advanced work and will require some study.

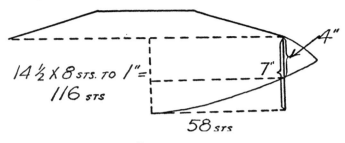

DIAGRAM 34.

WIDE, OFF-SHOULDER, CURVED NECKLINE

Measurement—Shoulder to shoulder—14½ inches
Stitch Gauge— 8 stitches to the inch
                    12 rows to the inch
Center of Neckline—7 inches below the tip of the shoulder and 4 inches down.

Method

As the neckline begins 7 inches from the tip of the shoulder and ends 4 inches from the tip of the shoulder, there are 3 inches in which to take off 58 stitches gradually.

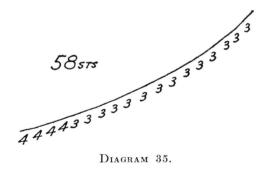

DIAGRAM 35.

12 rows to the inch times 3 inches = 36 rows, but we can only bind off every other row, so there are 18 rows in which to decrease. 18 into 58 goes 3 times and 4 over; that means there are 4 rows at the beginning where 4 stitches are bound off and 14 rows of 3s.

METHOD FOR WIDE, OFF-SHOULDER, CURVED NECKLINE

1. Knit to the center.
2. According to the stitch gauge, find the number of rows in the curve at the neck edge, then divide by 2 to learn the number of rows on which to decrease.
3. Divide the number of rows into the number of stitches to ascertain how many are to be bound off at one time.
4. Add any extra stitches, one stitch at a time, to the first decreases.
5. Knit the other half to correspond, only in reverse.

SLEEVE ENDING AT THE NECK EDGE

The cap of the sleeve is only partially completed. Decrease the cap, the same as *Chapter 15*, until it fits into the reduced armhole, 4 inches less than half the total armhole measurement.

SWEATERS WITHOUT SLEEVES
[a tight band across to keep the sweater from slipping]

Method

Measure the distance around the upperarm where the neckline ends. According to the width of the band desired, knit a piece *stretching* it to the desired length, so the strap will keep in position. When the sweater is completed, sew the straps in place and single-crochet tightly around the neck edge and the straps, on the right side, or if necessary, catch-stitch narrow elastic inside the neck edge and bands.

PROJECTS

1. Diagram and chart a wide, off-shoulder neckline.
    Measurements—Shoulder to shoulder—15 inches
    Stitch Gauge— 7 stitches to the inch
                          10 rows to the inch
    The neckline to start 6 inches down and 2 inches below
    the tip of the shoulder.
    Requires a little concentration—you can do it!

2. Check your answer on pages 248 and 249.

CHAPTER 26

DIFFERENT NECKLINES FOR EVENING SWEATERS

A WIDE, ON-SHOULDER OVAL NECKLINE

Measurement—Shoulder-to-shoulder—14½ inches
Stitch Gauge— 8 stitches to the inch
12 rows to the inch

Neckline to start 6 inches below the tip of the shoulder, using 2 shoulder slopes.

Note: If any part of the shoulder line is to be used, the shoulders must be diagrammed and charted.

Method

14½ inches times 8 stitches to the inch = 116 stitches.

8 stitches to the inch, therefore there are 6 slopes at the shoulder. See diagrams 36 and 37.

Knit halfway across the 116 stitches (58 stitches). Place the remaining 58 stitches on a stitch holder.

There are 12 rows to the inch, therefore 6 times 12 are 72 rows. Binding off every other row, means 36 rows on which to decrease.

As 14 stitches remain at the shoulder, 58 minus 14 stitches leaves 44 stitches to decrease in 36 rows. 44 stitches minus 35 rows—one of the 36 rows for the first bind-off—gives us 9 stitches and the rest decreased by knitting 2 together, every front row, at the neck edge, and finally the two, sevens at the shoulder.

The other side is completed similarly, only in reverse.

103

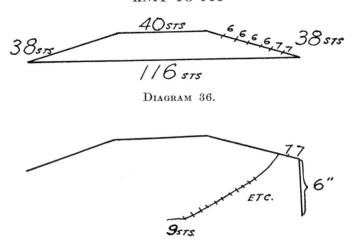

DIAGRAM 36.

DIAGRAM 37.

METHOD FOR WIDE, ON-SHOULDER NECKLINE

1.   Diagram and chart the shoulders.

2.   Knit to the center and subtract the stitches to be used at the shoulder to ascertain how many stitches to be decreased at the neckline.

3.   According to the stitch gauge, find the number of rows on which to decrease.

4.   Subtract the number of rows from the number of stitches to learn the number of stitches to bind off at the center.

5.   Knit 2 together, every front row, at the neck edge, until the shoulder stitches remain.

6.   Bind off the shoulder stitches.

7.   Knit the other side to correspond.

Note: Check the armhole measurement and, if necessary, knit even until the correct length.

ILLUSTRATION 16.

A WIDE, SQUARE, ON-SHOULDER NECKLINE

As for any type of neckline, measure the depth from the tip of the shoulder.

Measurements—Shoulder-to-shoulder—14½ inches

Stitch Gauge— 8 stitches to the inch

12 rows to the inch

The neckline starts 5 inches below the tip of the shoulder and uses 3 shoulder slopes. See diagram 38.

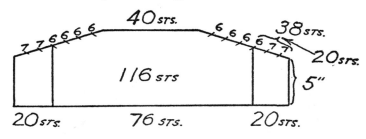

DIAGRAM 38.

Method

1. 14½ times 8 stitches to the inch is 116 stitches.
2. 8 stitches to the inch, therefore there are 6 steps for each shoulder. Using 3 slopes, there are 20 stitches, 40 for both shoulders.
3. 40 stitches from 116 leaves 76 stitches to bind off for the neckline.
4. Knit 20 stitches. Bind off 76 stitches.
5. Knit even on the 20 stitches until the armhole measurement is reached, then shape the shoulder.
6. Work the other side to correspond, only in reverse.

METHOD FOR WIDE, ON-SHOULDER NECKLINE

1. Bind off the center stitches.
2. Knit the left side to the shoulder.
3. Shape the shoulder.
4. Knit the right side to correspond, only in reverse.

PROJECTS

1. Diagram and chart a wide, on-shou'der, oval neckline using the same measurements and stitch gauge as the project in *Chapter 25*, the neckline to start 5 inches below the tip of the shoulder and using 2 shoulder slopes.
2. Diagram and chart a wide, square, on-shoulder neckline, using the same measurements and stitch gauge as #1, the neckline to start 6 inches below the tip of the shoulder and using 3 slopes.
3. Check the answers on pages 249 to 251.

CHAPTER 27

ATTACHED CAP SLEEVES ON SWEATERS AND BLOUSES

ACCENTS

IN THIS TYPE of sleeve, no armhole is actually knitted although it is necessary to figure the number of stitches that would be taken off at the armhole, and for the shaping of the shoulders.

Measurements

Shoulder to shoulder—14½ inches
Across the Back Underarm—17 inches
Length of Cap—2 inches from the tip of the shoulder
Armscye—18 inches
Stitch Gauge—8 stitches to the inch.

Note: The actual cap may be 1, 2, 3 inches or more in length and protrude straight out from the tip of the shoulder or it may hug the upper arm.

Follow diagram carefully.

Method

1. The across the back underarm measurement is 17 inches times 8 stitches to the inch = 136 stitches.
2. The shoulder-to-shoulder measurement is 14½ inches times 8 stitches to the inch = 116 stitches.
3. The underarm stitches, 136 minus the shoulder stitches 116, leaves 20 stitches, that is 10 from each side.
4. The length of the cap is 2 inches—8 stitches to the inch = 16 stitches. That is, 16 stitches to protrude beyond the shoulder stitches.

5. 16 stitches minus 10 stitches that were not taken off at the armscye leaves 6 stitches. See diagram 39.

6. As there should be a slight curve at the armhole edge 3 increases are made every other row, then 3 cast on at one time. We now have 16 stitches or 2 inches more than the tip of the shoulder.

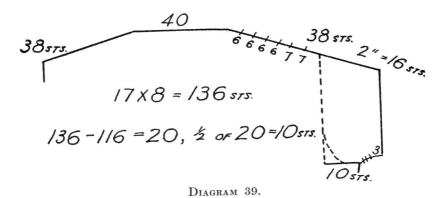

DIAGRAM 39.

A STRAIGHT CAP

If a straight cap from the shoulder is desired, knit even until the armscye measurement is reached, then bind off the extra 16 stitches and complete the shoulder as desired for the particular type of neckline.

Note: 1. The actual armscye will have to be gauged when measuring. Be sure it isn't too small.

2. Back and front low necklines are diagrammed in the same manner as previously.

CAP TO HUG THE UPPERARM

If the top of the cap is to hug the upperarm, the stitches should be bound off gradually according to the closeness desired. See diagram 40. 2 stitches are bound off, every other row,

8 times, that takes 16 rows at 12 rows to the inch, the decreasing is started 1¼ inches before the tip of the shoulder.

As the total armhole measurement is 18 inches, half is 9 inches minus 1¼ inches or 7¾ inches. That would give a sleeve width of 15½ inches. See diagram.

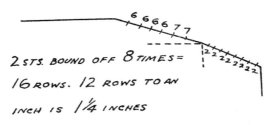

DIAGRAM 40.

METHOD FOR ATTACHED CAP SLEEVES

1. Decide the length of the cap from the shoulder and multiply by the stitch gauge.

2. Chart the top of the garment to find how many stitches should be taken off at the armhole.

3. Subtract the armhole stitches from the length of the cap stitches, to find how many stitches to add.

4. Add ½ an inch of stitches, one, every other row, for a slight curve at the underarm.

5. Add the rest of the stitches at the underarm.

6. Knit even for ½ the desired width of the cap sleeve.

PROJECTS

1. Using the measurements of *Chapter 25*, the across the back underarm measurement—18 inches and the stitch gauge—7 stitches to the inch, diagram and chart
   (a) A 3-inch cap straight out from the shoulder.
   (b) A 3-inch cap fitting at the upperarm.

2. File illustrations of evening sweaters according to:
   (a) Necklines
   (b) Sleeves

3. Check the answers on pages 251 and 252.

ILLUSTRATION 17.

ACCENTS THAT GIVE YOUR GARMENTS THAT DISTINCTIVE EXPENSIVE LOOK

FANCY GOLD AND SILVER EMBROIDERY using sequins, paillettes, bangle beads and seed pearls are very popular since non-tarnishable metallic threads have been established.

The design is often outlined with one or two strands of metallic thread couched or fastened down with overcast stitches. The centers are sometimes filled with large beads or seed pearls, sequins or other decorations connected by means of a back stitch and small bead. See Illustration 18.

When rows of sequins or paillettes are desired, buy them in strands, and fasten on to the design by means of overcast stitches.

Unattached paillettes may be used by fastening the first by means of a back stitch then thread the next through the center of the first and so on.

If one wishes to add sequins to a sweater or hat, use 2 yarns or threads, one finer than the other; thread the thin yarn with the sequins and distribute them at certain desired spaces, when knitting the 2 yarns at the same time.

Note: This allows heavier material to be used for the garment.

ILLUSTRATION 18.

TRANSFERRING DESIGNS ON FABRIC

As knitted material is easily stretched out of shape, it is necessary to sew either fine canvas or other fine material at the back.

Note: If needlepoint or cross stitch is used for the decoration, the canvas is attached at the front of the work.

Method

1. Mark the position of the design with small pins.
2. Transfer the design with a quick downward press. Be careful of smudging.
3. If making own design, carbon paper may be used in many instances.

4. For fine materials, trace the design on tissue paper, and baste on the right side. Remove the tissue paper after the design has been completed.

There are endless ways of decorating knits—crochet and daisy-knit flowers, appliqués of felt and other material, duplicate stitches, textile painting and monogramming to name some of them.

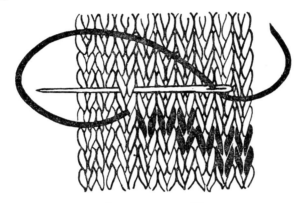

ILLUSTRATION 19.

DUPLICATE STITCH

If you are in doubt as how to apply some of the methods, I suggest you read my COMPLETE BOOK OF NEEDLE-CRAFT.

BUTTONS
#1 CROCHET

It is easier to work crochet over wooden forms rather than metal, because the work doesn't slip. Wooden molds may be purchased at notion counters—remember the added material adds greatly to the size.

Use a small crochet hook to insure a small stitch, the size depending upon the type of yarn.

Method

1. Chain 4 to 6 stitches and join with a slip stitch.
2. Single crochet in the ring (about 6 single crochets) until the ring is closed and the work is flat.
3. Mark the beginning of the round, and single crochet twice in each stitch.
4. Continue to increase as many times in each round as single crochet in #2.
5. When nearing the size of the mold, single crochet one round even.

Note: Must fit very tightly or will slip when worn.

6. Place the material over the mold, and decrease in each round, the same number of times you increased, more if necessary.

    Decrease as follows:

    Insert the hook in the chain, draw out the loop (do not finish the stitch) ; insert the hook in the next chain, draw out the loop (3 loops on the hook). Thread over and through the 3 loops on the hook.

7. Leave an end to fasten on the garment.

ILLUSTRATION 20.

#2 KNITTED

Metal moulds for knitted material may be obtained at notion departments and many Five-and-Tens.

Knit a piece of stockinette-stitch material, starting with 4 to 6 stitches, depending upon the weight of the yarn, and increase at the beginning and end of knit rows until wide enough, then work 4 to 6 rows even and decrease the same as the increases were done.

The directions for completing the button are given with the moulds.

#3 SINGLE CROCHET OVER PLASTIC RINGS

(a) Single crochet tightly and as closely as possible over the ring.

(b) Join.

(c) Turn the stitches toward the center and sew together.

(d) A bead, shell or rhinestone may be added to give added chic.

BELTS

Plastic rings of different sizes may be used instead of buckles for Belts. Both are covered with tight, single crochet stitches. The belt material should be sewn over Grosgrain ribbon to give it strength and a neat edge. If a wide belt is desired, catch stitch in the center to prevent rolling.

CHAPTER 28

ALTERATION OF HAND-KNIT AND MACHINE-KNIT GARMENTS

FOR ONE WHO desires to earn a livelihood in a special line of the knitting field, alterations could become a very lucrative business. Besides, anyone who handles hand-knits, designs herself, instructs, or knits for others, should know how to alter garments without ravelling them completely.

As we shall see in our next lesson, it is advisable to start all hand-knit skirts at the bottom, whether they are knitted on a circular needle, or in panels on straight needles. The correct tension of the stitch, the stitch gauge, is assured, by the time the important fitting areas [namely the hips and the waist] are reached.

I think we all realize that it is impossible to ravel any knitting from the beginning. No knitting can be pulled out backwards.

TO SHORTEN A HAND-KNIT SKIRT

If the skirt "cups", or "sits-out" at the back, it may be lifted and the extra length taken from the top. However, if the skirt fits satisfactorily, shorten in the following way.

Method

1. Mark the desired length of the skirt, which, no matter what fashion dictates, should meet individual needs.
2. Break a thread just above this length, the same as when snagging a stocking.
3. Pull out the thread as far as possible, before it breaks. The knit loops will remain facing downwards and will not pull out.

4. Using a #4 or #5 steel crochet hook, slip-stitch (crochet) in all the loops.

Note: #4 or #5 crochet hook is all right for all general purposes and much faster than using a knitting needle.

5. Continue to pull out the yarn and slip-stitch in the loops until they are all secured.
6. Single crochet around the bottom several times to prevent the skirt from rolling.

TO LENGTHEN A HAND-KNITTED SKIRT

Method

1. Break a thread near the bottom of the skirt, about 3 rows up.
2. Pick up the stitches on the same number circular needle as was used to knit the skirt, or a smaller size, then knit on the correct size. Pick up the stitches from the back so the loops will not be twisted.
3. Knit for the desired length.
4. Single crochet around the bottom several times and always on the right side, in each stitch and just a little tighter than the knitting.

Note: The following can only be done with stockinette stitch. The joining shows if one breaks a thread in ribbing.

TO SHORTEN OR LENGTHEN SLEEVES

Break a thread above the ribbing, at the necessary place to lengthen or shorten the sleeve, then knit down, adding the ribbing.

TO LENGTHEN A SWEATER FROM UNDERARM TO WAIST

Method

1. Undo the side seams for several inches above the ribbing.
2. Break a thread about 3 rows above the ribbing, either at the front or back.

3. Knit down the desired length, using the used yarn.
4. Decrease instead of increase at the waist for the ribbing.
5. Knit the other half to correspond and slip-stitch the seams.

REMODELLING MACHINE-KNIT GARMENTS

It is impossible to unravel machine-knit dresses and sweaters that are cut to shape.

Method

1. After the garment has been fitted and the correct position of the seams and hem marked, machine-stitch several times just inside the cutting line, so the material won't ravel.
2. Cut and sew on a machine, just like a woven fabric.
3. If any part has to be shortened, single crochet the same as a hand-knit.

PROJECT

Make a small piece of fabric of stockinette stitch. Break a thread and lengthen one inch.

CHAPTER 29

SKIRTS

Now WE HAVE arrived at one of the big reasons why women, with figures that don't fall into an exact pattern size, consider Hand-knits absolutely "out" for them. There have been too many protruding derrières and figure problems stressed. The fault rests with the instructor or designer, for, with a well-fitting foundation and correctly styled garment, any woman can look well in a hand-knit.

There are far too many people instructing in hand-knitting, who do not know the first thing about dress design, how to take measurements for knits, diagramming and charting, or correct styling to meet individual needs. Practically all their instructions are guesswork, through the use of only a knitting manual, where individual needs cannot be taken into consideration. I feel it is appalling the way some "knit shops" cut and hack hand-knits, especially ribbons. Oh yes, this is done, and in some instances, an exorbitant price is charged for altering and finishing.

FACTORS IN SKIRT STYLING

There are 4 factors to be considered in a well-fitting skirt.

1. The skirt should be wide enough at the hips to allow for comfortable sitting.

Every skirt should have extra width at the hip line no matter what style it is or for what type of figure it is made. This varies with the style, but a general rule is, the slimmer the lines, the greater the amount to be added. The reason for slim skirts "reaching up" when one is sitting, is because sufficient room isn't allowed for "spreading." It is the *width*, not the *length* that is at fault and no amount of length added will change it.

2. A skirt should allow for freedom of movement. Any garment should be considered in the light of sitting, standing and walking.

3. The style should be suited to the purpose, day, afternoon, evening, etc.

4. The grain, that is, the rows of knitting, should run horizontally around the figure and straight up and down.

STRAIGHT SKIRTS

Four measurements are necessary.

1. Waist—this is taken with 2 fingers eased between the tape and the body. This is one measurement that fits. See *Chapter 3.*

2. Hips—this is not the actual hip measurements, but around the fullest part, 7 to 9 inches down, the same distance from the waist all the way around. Do not pull the tape tightly, but eased, as one does when measuring for a pattern. One has to be particularly careful, especially for a larger person with a "tummy." We do not want the skirt to draw in front.

3. Width at the Bottom—this varies. The necessary hip measurement may be used, in which case a slit or pleat is necessary. A wider bottom is still considered a straight skirt, but no slit is required.

Measurements for Straight Skirt

Waist—28 inches.
Hip—38 inches, 9 inches below the waist.
Length—31 inches, 1 inch allowed for crocheting, so 30
            inches is the knitted length.
Width at the Bottom—52 inches.
Stitch Gauge—6 stitches to the inch.
Note: 4 inches is added to the hip measurement to allow for "spread."

Method

Waist—28 inches times 6 stitches to the inch = 168 stitches, the nearest number divisible by 10 is 170 stitches.

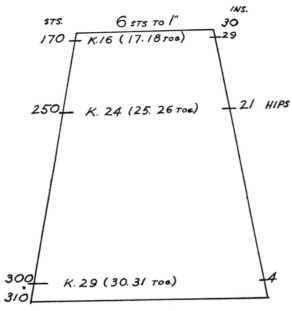

DIAGRAM 41.

6 sts to the inch

Sts		Ins	
170		30	
170	K.16 (17.18 tog.)	29	last inch even
180	K.17 (18.19 tog.)	28	
190	K.18 (19.20 tog.)	27	
200	K.19 (20.21 tog.)	26	
210	K.20 (21.22 tog.)	25	
220	K.21 (22.23 tog.)	24	
230	K.22 (23.24 tog.)	23	
240	K.23 (24.25 tog.)	22	
250	K.24 (25.26 tog.)	21	Hips
260	K.25 (26.27 tog.)	18	
270	K.26 (27.28 tog.)	15	
280	K.27 (28.29 tog.)	12	
290	K.28 (29.30 tog.)	8	
300	K.29 (30.31 tog.)	4	
310			

DIAGRAM 42.

Hips—38 inches plus 4 inches = 42 inches, times 6 is 252 stitches, the nearest 10 is 250 stitches.

Width at the Bottom—52 inches times 6 = 312 stitches, nearest 10 is 310 stitches.

DECREASING FROM THE BOTTOM TO THE HIP

310 stitches minus 250 stitches leaves 60 stitches to be reduced evenly to the hips. Decreasing 10 stitches at a time, there are 6 decreases.

31 inches is the finished length, but 30 inches the knitted length, therefore, the hip, 9 inches down is 21 inches. 21 inches to make 6 decreases of 10 stitches. 6 into 21 goes 3 times and 3 inches over. Therefore, the first 3 decreases are at every 4 inches and the next 3 are 3 inches apart. Follow diagram.

HOW TO REDUCE

In 310 stitches there are 31 tens to be reduced to 30 tens. This is done by knitting 29 and the 30th and 31st stitches together all the way around.

The next number is automatically reduced 1 stitch, so the next decrease is knit 28 stitches and the 29th and 30th together and so on for the remainder of the decreasing.

HIPS TO THE WAIST

250 stitches at the hips minus 170 stitches at the waist = 80 stitches or 8 decreases of 10. Follow diagram 41.

Note: The last decrease is never at the waist line. Allow ½ an inch or 1 inch even.

METHOD FOR STRAIGHT SKIRT

1. Deduct 1 inch from the length for the crocheting at the top and bottom.

2. Multiply the waist, the necessary hip measurement and the width at the bottom by the stitch gauge.

3. Use the nearest numbers, divisible by 10, to simplify the charting.

4. Subtract the necessary stitches at the hip from the stitches at the bottom, then from the hip to the waist.

5. Divide by 10 to learn how many decreases are to be made.

6. Divide the number of decreases into the number of inches from the bottom to the hip and from the hip to the waist to know where to decrease.

Note: Any extra inches to be added, 1 inch at a time, to the decreases nearest the bottom and then the hips.

Note: 1. A 31-inch length skirt may appear long, but I have taken varying lengths to suit individual needs and any changes in fashion as will be seen in *Chapter 30.*

2. No matter what stretch has to be allowed for certain materials, the garment must be charted correctly according to measurements, and when measuring, allow for the stretch.

PROJECT

1. Diagram and chart a straight skirt with the following measurements:

   Waist—29 inches.

   Hip—39 inches, 9 inches down.

   Length of skirt—31 inches, allow 1 inch for crocheting.

   Width at the bottom—10 inches more than the hip measurement—53 inches.

   Stitch gauge—6 stitches to the inch.

2. Check the answer on pages 253 and 254.

STRAIGHT TWO-PIECE SKIRT ON MACHINE

The same measurements are used as in diagrams 41 and 42. For a well-fitting, 2-piece skirt, the decreases must be made across a row.

Follow the diagrams.

Bottom—½ of 310 stitches = 155 stitches
Hips   —½ of 250 stitches = 125 stitches
Waist —½ of 170 stitches = 85 stitches

The decreases are exactly the same as for working on a circular needle, except that ½ the stitches will be taken off each time, which means that not 10 but 5 stitches are decreased at a time, allowing, of course, rows for inches.

Note: Extra stitches should be allowed for seam allowances. I suggest 2 or 3 extra stitches at each side.

The first decrease is K. 29, then 30 and 31 together, and so on. However, for a better fit, the first 29 stitches may be split and have K. 15, then 16 and 17 together. At the end, there will be K. 14, and so on up the skirt, allowing one fewer stitch between every decrease.

HOW TO DECREASE ACROSS A ROW

1. Work extra row using a contrasting color where decreases have to be made.
2. Drop the work from the machine.
3. Fold so the main-color stitches stand out.
4. Replace on the machine, putting 2 stitches on one needle where decreases are required, being sure all latches are open.
5. Pull out contrasting color.

INCREASING ACROSS A ROW

Increase in the same way but leave a space open for extra stitch.

See answers on pages 253 and 254.

CHAPTER 30

STRAIGHT SKIRTS WITH DIFFERENT STITCH GAUGES AND LENGTHS

Measurements—the same as for previous straight skirt.
Length of Skirt—28 inches.
Knitted Length—27 inches.

Stitch Gauge—7 stitches to the inch.
Waist—28 inches times 7 stitches to the inch = 196 stitches, nearest 10, 200 stitches.
Hip—38 inches plus 4 inches = 42 inches, times 7 stitches to the inch is 294 stitches, nearest 10, 290 stitches for the hip (8 inches down).
Width at the Bottom—52 inches times 7 stitches to the inch = 364 stitches, nearest 10, 360 stitches.
Diagrams 43 and 44 are self-explanatory. Follow closely.

Measurements—the same as for previous example.

Length of Skirt—27 inches.
Knitted Length—26 inches.

Stitch Gauge—8 stitches to the inch.
Waist—28 inches times 8 stitches to the inch = 224 stitches, nearest 10, 220 stitches.
Hip—38 inches plus 4 inches = 42 inches times 8 stitches to the inch is 336 stitches, 340 stitches for the hip (9 inches down).
Width at the Bottom—52 inches times 8 stitches to the inch is 416 stitches, nearest 10, 420 stitches. Follow diagrams 45 and 46.

125

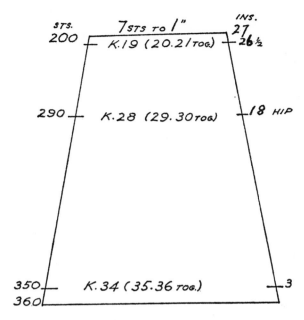

DIAGRAM 43.

<u>7 sts to the inch</u>

Sts		Ins	
200		27	last 1/2 inch even
200	K.19 (20.21 tog.)	26 1/2	
210	K.20 (21.22 tog.)	26	
220	K.21 (22.23 tog.)	25	
230	K.22 (23.24 tog.)	24	
240	K.23 (24.25 tog.)	23	
250	K.24 (25.26 tog.)	22	
260	K.25 (26.27 tog.)	21	
270	K.26 (27.28 tog.)	20	
280	K.27 (28.29 tog.)	19	
290	K.28 (29.30 tog.)	18	Hip
300	K.29 (30.31 tog.)	16	
310	K.30 (31.32 tog.)	14	
320	K.31 (32.33 tog.)	12	
330	K.32 (33.34 tog.)	9	
340	K.33 (34.35 tog.)	6	
350	K.34 (35.36 tog.)	3	
360			

DIAGRAM 44.

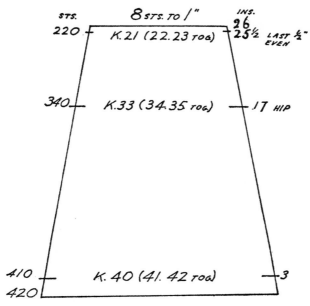

DIAGRAM 45.

8 sts to the inch

Sts		Ins	
220		26	last 1/2 inch even
220	K.21 (22.23 tog.)	25 1/2	
230	K.22 (23.24 tog.)	25	
240	K.23 (24.25 tog.)	24 1/2	
250	K.24 (25.26 tog.)	24	
260	K.25 (26.27 tog.)	23 1/2	
270	K.26 (27.28 tog.)	23	
280	K.27 (28.29 tog.)	22 1/2	
290	K.28 (29.30 tog.)	22	
300	K.29 (30.31 tog.)	21	
310	K.30 (31.32 tog.)	20	
320	K.31 (32.33 tog.)	19	
330	K.32 (33.34 tog.)	18	
340	K.33 (34.35 tog.)	17	Hip
350	K.34 (35.36 tog.)	15	
360	K.35 (36.37 tog.)	13	
370	K.36 (37.38 tog.)	11	
380	K.37 (38.39 tog.)	9	
390	K.38 (39.40 tog.)	7	
400	K.39 (40.41 tog.)	5	
410	K.40 .(41.42 tog.)	3	
420			

DIAGRAM 46.

PROJECT

Diagram and chart 2 straight skirts.

Measurements—the same as for the previous project in *Chapter 29*.

Waist—29 inches.

Hip—39 inches at the fullest part (9 inches below the waist).

Length of skirt—31 inches.

Stitch Gauge—7 and 8 stitches to the inch.

MACHINE-KNIT STRAIGHT SKIRT IN TWO PIECES
With open darts, starting at the top

This method has six edges for increasing.

Measurements

Waist—28 inches

Hip—38 inches

Length—30 inches

Stitch Gauge—6 sts. to the inch

½ of Waist, 28 inches, is 14 inches.

½ of necessary hip, 42 inches, is 21 inches.

Note: When Sewing, darts are made where necessary, but generally over ⅓ is allowed at the center for knitting.

1. 14 inches × by 6 sts. to the inch = 84 sts. (waist).

2. 21 inches × by 6 sts. to the inch = 126 sts. (hip).

3. The difference—126 sts. minus 84 means 42 sts. to be added—2 sts. at each dart and 1 st. at each side, making 6 increases.

4. 6 into 42 sts. goes 7 times, therefore, 7 increases altogether.

5. Increase both in darts and sides, every inch, 7 times, then work straight for the desired length on the 126 sts. See diagram 46a.

Note: No seam allowances were allowed at the sides.

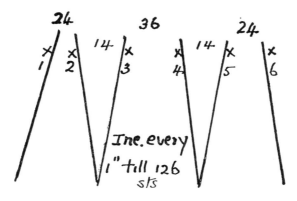

DIAGRAM 46A.

Method

Three balls are necessary for this procedure.

Starting from left to right, cast on 24 sts.; leave 14 sts. at rest; cast on 36 sts. for the center; 14 sts. at rest; cast on 24 sts. 126 sts., from side to side, are in operation.

Work 1 inch even, then increase on all 6 sides, every inch, until all the spaces are filled and there are 126 sts.

Knit evenly for the desired length.

Knit 2 similar pieces.

See answers on pages 255 and 256.

MORE COMPLICATED BUT BETTER WAY TO MAKE DARTS

Actually the darts shouldn't be quite so long or curve as much as the side shaping, although the above directions will suffice.

Second Method

Allow about 5 inches for each dart. So, increasing for darts, every inch for 5 inches, requires 5 × 4, which = 20 sts.

42 sts. minus 20 sts. leaves 22 sts. for both sides, or 11 for each side. The hip is 9 inches down from the waist, so increase every ¾ inch, 11 times at the sides, until you have 126 sts.

CHAPTER 31

FLARED SKIRTS

THE FULLNESS that is added at the hips of a flared skirt depends upon the amount of flare from the bottom to the hips. Some flared skirts may appear to fit around the hips, but even then, there must be at least 2 inches more allowed for the actual hip measurement. Generally speaking, the smaller the flare, the greater the amount added at the hips. For example, if the width at the bottom is only 15 inches more than the actual hip measurement, this is a semi-straight skirt and 4 inches more than the hip measurement should be added. For small figures, it may be desirous to have a loose-fitting skirt from the bottom to the waist and the decreasing figured accordingly—even all the way from the bottom to the waist.

LENGTH OF SKIRT

No matter what the prevailing fashion, the length of a skirt should be determined by the figure, especially the ankles and the legs. 16 or 18 inches from the floor is not suitable for everyone. Mid-calf is a good length for older women.

1. FLARED SKIRT WITH EVEN FLARE TO THE HIPS

We shall again use the measurements that were used for the straight skirt.

Waist—28 inches.
Hips—38 inches.
Length—31 inches.
Width at the Bottom—60 inches.
Stitch Gauge—6 stitches to the inch.

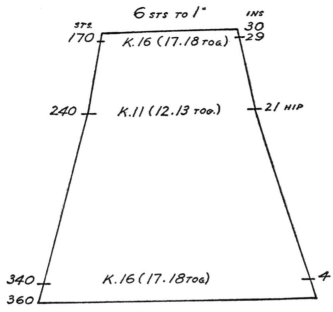

DIAGRAM 47.

6 sts to the inch

Sts		Ins	
170		30	
170	K.16 (17.18 tog.)	29	last inch even
180	K.17 (18.19 tog.)	28	
190	K.18 (19.20 tog.)	27	
200	K.19 (20.21 tog.)	26	
210	K.20 (21.22 tog.)	25	
220	K.21 (22.23 tog.)	24	
230	K.22 (23.24 tog.)	23	
240	K.11 (12.13 tog.)	21	Hip
260	K.12 (13.14 tog.)	18	
280	K.13 (14.15 tog.)	15	
300	K.14 (15.16 tog.)	12	
320	K.15 (16.17 tog.)	8	
340	K.16 (17.18 tog.)	4	
360			

DIAGRAM 48.

In our example, 20 inches were added to the width at the bottom, so only 2 inches more than the actual hip measurement are necessary, as there is sufficient width below the hips.

Method

Waist—28 inches times 6 stitches to the inch = 168 stitches, even 10 is 170 stitches.

Hips—38 inches plus 2 inches = 40 inches times 6 is 240 stitches.

Width at the Bottom—40 inches plus 20 inches = 60 inches times 6 = 360 stitches. Follow diagrams 47 and 48.

Note: 1. If many stitches have to be decreased, it is better to decrease 20 stitches in one round rather than 10 stitches.

2. To take off 20 stitches, the number must be divisible by 20, if not, reduce 10 stitches first.

In 360, there are 18 twenties. For 340, we require 17 twenties, therefore, every 18 stitches have to be decreased 1 stitch. That is, knit 16 stitches, then knit the 17th and 18th together.

As in the straight skirt, the number of stitches between each decrease automatically decreases 1 stitch at a time.

See the straight skirt for the method of ascertaining the position of decreases.

DECREASES FROM THE BOTTOM TO THE HIPS

The difference in the number of stitches from the bottom to the hips is 120 stitches or 6 decreases of 20 stitches. 6 into 21 goes 3 inches with 3 inches over; therefore, the first 3 decreases are at every 4 inches and the remainder at 3 inches to the hips.

DECREASES FROM THE HIPS TO THE WAIST

240 minus 170 stitches leaves 70; therefore, there are 7 decreases of 10 stitches, so decrease every inch, 7 times, with the last inch even.

PROJECT

1. Diagram and chart a flared skirt using measurements as for *Chapter 30*, allowing 1 inch for crocheting. The width at the bottom is 61 inches, which is 20 inches more than the necessary hip measurement of 39 inches plus 2. The stitch gauge is 6 stitches to the inch.
2. Check the answer on pages 257 and 258.

CHAPTER 32

FLARED SKIRTS WITH DIFFERENT STITCH GAUGES AND LENGTHS

As FLARED SKIRTS should never be knitted of heavy material, we shall not consider 5 stitches to the inch.

#1. *Measurements*—the same as for *Chapter 31*, allowing a 15-inch flare.

> Length of Skirt—28 inches.
> Knitted Length—27 inches.

Stitch Gauge—7 stitches to the inch.

Method

Follow diagrams 49 and 50.

Waist—28 inches times 7 stitches to the inch = 196 stitches, 200 stitches nearest 10.

Hip—38 inches plus 4 inches = 42 inches times 7 stitches to the inch, or 294 stitches, nearest 10, 290 stitches (9 inches down).

Width at the Bottom—42 inches plus 15 inches = 57 inches times 7 stitches to the inch or 399 stitches, nearest 10, 400 stitches.

400 stitches at the bottom, minus 290 stitches at the hips leaves 110 stitches, therefore, there are 5 decreases of 20 stitches and one decrease of 10 stitches to the hips.

6 times to decrease into 18 inches goes 3, therefore, there are 3 inches between each decrease to the hips.

The stitches from the hips to the waist are taken off in 10's, 9 decreases altogether.

Note: Always check the stitch gauge at the hips.

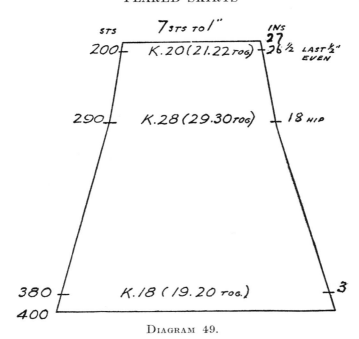

DIAGRAM 49.

7 sts to the inch

Sts		Ins	
200		27	
200	K.19 (20.21 tog.)	26	1/2-last 1/2 inch even
210	K.20 (21.22 tog.)	26	
220	K.21 (22.23 tog.)	25	
230	K.22 (23.24 tog.)	24	
240	K.23 (24.25 tog.)	23	
250	K.24 (25.26 tog.)	22	
260	K.25 (26.27 tog.)	21	
270	K.26 (27.28 tog.)	20	
280	K.27 (28.29 tog.)	19	
290	K.28 (29.30 tog.)	18	Hip
300	K.14 (15.16 tog.)	15	
320	K.15 (16.17 tog.)	12	
340	K.16 (17.18 tog.)	9	
360	K.17 (18.19 tog.)	6	
380	K.18 (19.20 tog.)	3	
400			

DIAGRAM 50.

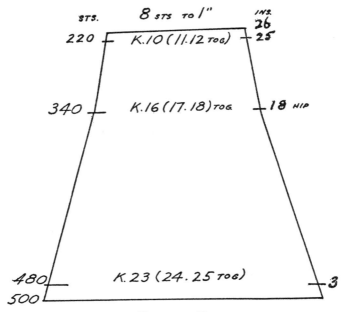

DIAGRAM 51.

8 sts to the inch

Sts		Ins	
220		26	
220	K.10 (11.12 tog.)	25	Last inch even
240	K.11 (12.13 tog.)	24	
260	K.12 (13.14 tog.)	23	
280	K.13 (14.15 tog.)	22	
300	K.14 (15.16 tog.)	21	
320	K.15 (16.17 tog.)	20	
340	K.16 (17.18 tog.)	18	Hip
360	K.17 (18.19 tog.)	16	
380	K.18 (19.20 tog.)	14	
400	K.19 (20.21 tog.)	12	
420	K.20 (21.22 tog.)	10	
440	K.21 (22.23 tog.)	8	
460	K.22 (23.24 tog.)	6	
480	K.23 (24.25 tog.)	3	
500			

DIAGRAM 52.

#2.   *Measurements*—the same as previously.

> Length of Skirt—27 inches.
> Knitted Length—26 inches.

The flare is released toward the bottom so 4 inches is added to the hip measurement.
Stitch Gauge—8 stitches to the inch.

Method

Waist—28 inches times 8 stitches to the inch = 224 stitches, 220 stitches is the nearest 10.

Hips—38 inches plus 4 inches = 42 inches, times 8 stitches to the inch or 336 stitches, 340 stitches is the nearest 10 (8 inches down).

Bottom of the Skirt—42 inches plus 20 inches = 62 inches, times 8 stitches to the inch or 496 stitches, 500 stitches is the nearest 10.

Study diagrams 51 and 52.

PROJECTS

1. Using previous measurements and 7 and 8 stitches to the inch gauges, adding 15 inches for 7 stitches to the inch and 20 inches for 8 stitches to the inch, chart the two flared skirts.

2. Check the answers on pages 259 to 263.

CHAPTER 33

GORED SKIRTS

A GORED SKIRT in hand-knitting is not worked in separate pieces, except for ribbon knits—these we shall discuss later. The effect of gores is achieved by means of purl stitches, 1 or 2, as desired, between each gore.

Gored skirts may have many numbers of gores, 4, 6, 8, 10, and more, depending upon the effect desired, the width at the bottom and individual needs. Again it must be remembered that the figure is very important. A long, thin person certainly shouldn't have many narrow gores, or, on the other hand, a large person shouldn't have wide gores, especially around the body—this emphasizes width.

A gored skirt may or may not fit closely around the hips. As for other skirts, 2 to 4 inches are always necessary and more if desired.

Note: Test with a tape measure when measuring the necessary width at the bottom, remembering that the finer the material, the greater the fullness may be.

Measurements

Waist—28 inches.
Length—31 inches minus 1 inch for crochet.
Hips—38 inches (9 inches down).
Width at the bottom—76 inches with 12 panels or gores.
Stitch Gauge—6 stitches to the inch.

As this gored skirt is for an average figure, we shall make it fitting from the hips to the waist and use 12 panels with 2 purled stitches between.

Method

Waist—28 inches times 6 stitches to the inch = 168 stitches, 12 gores into 168 goes 14 times, therefore, each gore has 12 knit stitches with purl 2 between.

Hips—a full skirt, therefore, 2 inches added to the hip measurement. 38 plus 2 inches = 40 inches, times 6 stitches to the inch is 240 stitches. There are 12 panels, therefore, 12 into 240 goes 20 times, which means that at the hip, the gores have K. 18 with P. 2 between.

Width at the Bottom—76 inches times 6 stitches to the inch is 456. 12 into 456 stitches goes 38 times, therefore, there are K. 36 stitches in each gore with P. 2 between.

Note: If the number of stitches allocated at different points do not divide evenly into the number of panels, take the nearest number that will. Follow diagrams 53 and 54.

BOTTOM TO THE HIPS

From the bottom of the skirt to the hips, the knits have to be reduced from 36 to 18, that is, 18 stitches in each gore. 2 stitches are taken off at one time, so there will be 9 decreases. 9 decreases into 21 inches goes twice and 3 inches over. Therefore, there will be 3 decreases every 3 inches, and 6 decreases, 2 inches.

Note: Always decrease by K. 1, K. 2 together at the beginning and K. 2 together, K. 1 the last 3 stitches.

HIPS TO THE WAIST

From the hips to the waist, we have to decrease 18 to 12, which means 6 stitches. See diagram 53. Reduce 1 stitch at a time, first at one side then at the other, every inch.

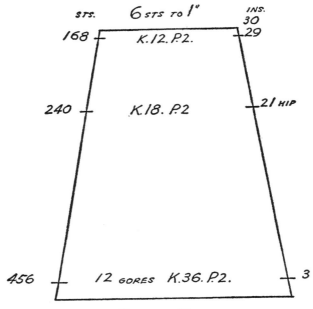

DIAGRAM 53.

6 sts to the inch

Sts		Ins	
168		30	
168	K.12.P.2.	29	last inch even
		28	
		27	
		26	
		25	
		23	
240	K.18.P.2.	21	Hip
		19	
		17	
		15	
		13	
		11	
		9	
		6	
		3	
456	12 gores – K.36.P.2.		

DIAGRAM 54.

METHOD FOR GORED SKIRTS

1.   Decide the number of gores.

2.   Multiply the waist measurement by the number of stitches to the inch and use the nearest number of stitches that will divide by the number of gores.

3.   Add the necessary number of inches to the hip measurement (according to fit desired and the width at the bottom) and multiply by the number of stitches to the inch, then use the nearest number divisible by the number of gores.

4.   Multiply the width at the bottom by the stitches to the inch and use the nearest number divisible by the number of gores.

5.   Divide the number of gores into the number of stitches as at the waist, hips and bottom to find the number of stitches in each gore at those points.

6.   Subtract the number of stitches in each gore at the hips from the stitches in each gore at the bottom to learn the number of stitches to decrease.

7.   Subtract the number of stitches in each gore at the waist from the number of stitches at the hips to learn the number to decrease.

8.   Divide the number of stitches to decrease into the number of inches. (a) From the bottom to the hips. (b) From the hips to the waist, to learn where to decrease.

PROJECTS

1.   Using the measurements from the previous *Chapter*, diagram and chart a 12-gored skirt with P. 2 between, width at the bottom—76 inches and 2 inches added at the hips. The Stitch Gauge—6 stitches to the inch.

2.   Check answers on pages 264 and 265.

CHAPTER 34

GORED SKIRTS WITH DIFFERENT
STITCH GAUGES AND LENGTHS

IN A WIDE gored skirt, it may be necessary to decrease more than 2 stitches in each gore at one time. In which case, knit 2 together in the center as well as at the beginning and end of each gore.

#1. *Measurements*

> Waist—28 inches.
> Hips—38 inches (9 inches down) 2 extra inches added.
> Width at the Bottom—80 inches, 8 gores with Purl 2 between.
> Length of Skirt—31 inches.
> Knitted Length—30 inches.
> Stitch Gauge—7 stitches to the inch.

Method

Waist—28 inches times 7 stitches to the inch = 196 stitches. There are 8 gores so 200 stitches are necessary. 8 into 200 goes 25 times, so there are K. 23 with P. 2 stitches between.

Hips—a full skirt, so only 2 inches are added to the hip measurement. 38 inches plus 2 inches = 40 inches, times 7 stitches to the inch makes 280 stitches. 8 gores into 280 stitches is 35, so there are K. 33 and P. 2 between each gore.

Width at the Bottom—80 inches times 7 stitches to the inch = 560 stitches. 8 gores into 560 is 70 times, therefore K. 68 and P. 2 between, for each gore. See diagrams 55 and 56.

As so many stitches have to be reduced from the bottom to the hips, it is advisable to decrease 3 stitches at a time in each gore, and 1 stitch each time from the hips to the waist.

The first decrease at the bottom is as follows: K. 1, K. 2 together, K. 30, K. 2 together, K. 30, K. 2 together, K. 1.

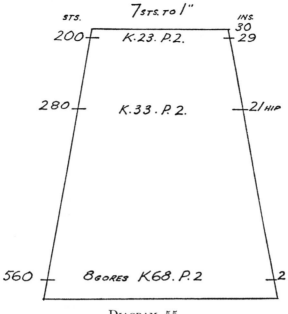

DIAGRAM 55.

7 sts to the inch

Sts		Ins	
		30	
200	K.23.P.2.	29	last inch even
		28½	
		28	
	10 decreases of 1 st	27½	
		27	
		26	
		25	
		24	
		23	
		22	
280	K.33.P.2.	21	Hip
	1 decrease of 2 sts	20	
		19	
		18	
	11 decreases of 3 sts	16	
		14	
		12	
		10	
		8	
		6	
		4	
		2	
560 -8 gores - K.68.P.2.			

DIAGRAM 56.

#2. *Measurements*

> Waist—28 inches.
> Hips—38 inches (9 inches down) 2 extra inches added.
> Width at the Bottom—76 inches with 6 gores and P. 1 between.
> Length of Skirt—28 inches.
> Knitted Length—27 inches.
> Stitch Gauge—8 stitches to the inch.

Method

Waist—28 inches times 8 stitches to the inch = 224 stitches, to be divisible by 6, is 222 stitches. 6 into 222 goes 37 times, i.e., K. 36, P. 1.

Hips—38 inches plus 2 inches = 40 inches, times 8 stitches to the inch is 320 stitches. To be divisible by 6 is 318 stitches. 6 into 318 goes 53 stitches, i.e., K. 52, P. 1.

Width at the Bottom—76 inches times 8 stitches to the inch = 608 stitches, 606 stitches divided by 6 is 101, i.e., K. 100, P. 1.

DECREASES FROM THE BOTTOM TO THE HIPS

100 stitches at the bottom, minus 52 stitches at the hips means 48 stitches to be reduced in each gore, i.e., 12 decreases of 4 stitches in each panel. The first decrease to be as follows: K. 1, K. 2 together, K. 30, K. 2 together, K. 30, K. 2 together, K.30, K. 2 together, K. 1 and so on for the others.

DECREASES FROM THE HIPS TO THE WAIST

52 stitches minus 36 stitches means 16 stitches to be reduced in each gore, i.e., 2 stitches each time (8 decreases). See diagrams 57 and 58.

Note: See *Chapter 37* for Machine-Knit Gored Skirts.

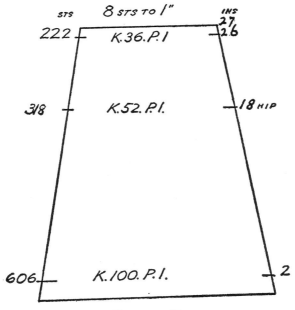

DIAGRAM 57.

<u>8 sts to the inch</u>

Sts		Ins	
222		27	
222	K.36.P.1.	26	last inch even
		25	
		24	
	2 decreases in each	23	
	gore	22	
		21	
		20	
		19	
318	K.52.P.1.	18	Hip
		17	
	12 decreases	16	
		15	
	4 decreases in each	14	
	gore	13	
		12	
		10	
		8	
		6	
		4	
		2	
606	K.100.P.1.		

DIAGRAM 58.

PROJECTS

1. Using the same measurements as for the previous lesson, diagram and chart:

   (a) An 8-gored skirt with P. 2 between, 80 inches wide at the bottom and 7 stitches to the inch, fitted at the hips.

   (b) A 6-gored skirt with P. 1 between, 76 inches wide at the bottom and 7 stitches to the inch, fitted at the hips.

2. Check answers on pages 266 to 269.

CHAPTER 35

PLEATED SKIRTS

KNITTED PLEATED SKIRTS are really not composed of pleats in the usual sense of the term. A number of knit and purl ribs are used, the number of stitches per inch determines the size of the ribs.

There are several important factors to consider when knitting a pleated skirt:

1. In a pleated or ribbed skirt, no crocheting is required, so the actual skirt length is taken into consideration when diagramming.

2. In order for the entire skirt to look pleated, unlike stripes, extra material must be allowed at the hip line. This varies from at least 4 inches.

3. The same applies to the waist—2 to 4 inches or more than the measurement are required.

4. The number of stitches for the width at the bottom of the skirt should be 76 inches or more, depending upon the width of the rib and the type of material. The finer the material, the greater the width may be.

Note: 1. A good criterion is that the width at the bottom should be approximately twice the hip measurement.

2. The narrower the rib, the narrower the skirt appears to be.

3. Pleats of K. 2, P. 2, and K. 3, P. 3 are better decreased the same as flared skirts, at regular intervals. I suggest you diagram this type of skirt from the waist down, to be sure the ribs come even at the top.

Measurements

Waist—28 inches plus 2 inches is 30 inches.

Hips—38 inches plus 4 inches is 42 inches (9 inches down).

Width at the Bottom—76 inches.

Length—31 inches, no allowance for crocheting.

Pleats or ribs—2 inches wide, 7 stitches to the inch, is 14 stitches.

Stitch Gauge—7 stitches to the inch.

Method

BOTTOM OF THE SKIRT

76 inches times 7 stitches to the inch = 532 stitches. 14 knit stitches and 14 purl stitches make 28 stitches. 28 into 532 goes 19 times, therefore, there are 19 knit ribs and 19 purl ribs, making 38 ribs altogether.

Hips—38 inches plus 4 inches = 42 inches times 7 stitches to the inch is 294 stitches, which must be divisible by 38 ribs. 38 doesn't go evenly into 294, so 304 stitches are used. 38 into 304 goes 8 times, i.e., K. 8, P. 8 at the hips.

Waist—28 inches plus 2 inches is 30 inches times 7 stitches to the inch is 210 stitches. 19 into 210 goes 11 and 1 stitch over, so we use the number 209 stitches and have K. 6 and P. 5 at the waist.

Note: If the number doesn't divide evenly, take the nearest number that will.

FROM THE BOTTOM TO THE HIPS—DECREASING

Since there are 19 ribs, the decreasing may be 19 or 38 stitches at one time. If only the knits are decreased, the number is 19 and the same with the purls. If both the knits and the purls are decreased, the number is 38 stitches.

14 stitches in each rib at the bottom, minus 8 stitches at the hips means 6 decreases both in the knit and purl ribs. A better-fitting skirt will result if the decreases are made gradually, first in the knits then in the purls, allowing 12 decreases to the hips.

Follow the diagrams for the decreases.

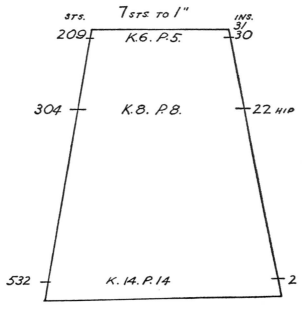

STS.   7 STS. TO 1"   INS.
                                     31
209   K.6. P.5.   30

304   K.8. P.8.   22 HIP

532   K. 14. P. 14.   2

DIAGRAM 59.

7 sts to the inch

Sts		Ins	
		31	
209		30	last inch even
209	K.6.P.5.	29	
		28	
	2 decreases in. knits	26	
	3 decreases in purls.	24	
304	K.8.P.8.	22	Hip
		21	
		20	
		18	
		16	
		14	
	19 knit ribs and 19 purl	12	
	ribs.	10	
		8	
		6	
		4	
		2	
532	K.14.P.14.		

DIAGRAM 60.

METHOD FOR PLEATED SKIRT

1. Multiply the width at the bottom by the number of stitches per inch. [Must be divisible by the combined knit and purl stitches of each rib.]

2. Hips—Add the necessary allowance of at least 4 inches to the hip measurement and multiply by the stitch gauge; the number must be divisible by the total number of ribs.

3. Waist—Add the necessary allowance to the waist measurement times the number of stitches to the inch. The number must be divisible by half the total number of ribs.

4. Subtract the number of stitches in each rib at the hip from the stitches in each rib at the bottom to know how many to decrease—similarly from the hips to the waist.

5. Divide the number of decreases into the inches, (a) from the bottom to the hips, (b) from the hips to the waist, to know where to decrease.

PROJECTS

1. Using the same measurements as for previous *Chapter*, diagram and chart:
   Pleated skirt with pleats 2 inches wide and 76 inches, the width at the bottom. Stitch Gauge—7 sts. to the inch.
2. Check the answer on pages 270 and 271.

MACHINE-KNIT PLEATED SKIRTS

Each pleat is knitted separately and put together afterwards, therefore too narrow ribs should not be used. These are diagrammed on the same principle as a gored skirt, decreasing on each side, and every other panel turned, so there must be an even number of panels, 14, 16, 18, etc.

One must remember, too, that manufacturers' large machines are not as limited as hand-knitting machines, but the results may even be better. Generally, in cheap, pleated-machine knits, the skirts are much too narrow.

RIBBON KNITS

WE MUST THANK A group of Parisian designers who originated knitting with ribbon, and discovered its durability, versatility and elegance. It is remarkable how the different types of ribbon with their silky finish lend themselves to a variety of textures and patterns, and are adaptable for all occasions, for business, for the cocktail hour and the ballroom. If you are one of the lucky ones and have a ribbon sheath or suit in your wardrobe, you know the pleasure and satisfaction of wearing one of the most luxurious, most crease-resistant packables.

The actual cost of the material is a mere fraction of a finished garment made of material of similar calibre, and has that envied couturier look that is so very, very expensive and only sold at élite stores or exclusive boutiques.

Today there are several types of ribbon used for ribbon knits. There are rayon, rayon and silk combined, rayon and silk with a metallic thread through the center, and all-silk organdy ribbon. Some have woven, others have fused edges.

Knitting with ribbon takes practice as it is quite different from ordinary knitting, but once the technique is acquired, a garment may be made more quickly than with other materials. This, of course, excludes bulky knits. Large needles are used, so fewer stitches are necessary. However, I consider ribbon knits exacting to make in their knitting, blocking, finishing and their final pressing.

METHOD OF KNITTING

The ribbon should be kept flat on the needle and worked very loosely, allowing considerable slack. So there will be no strain, unwind the ribbon a couple of yards each time—do not pull out too much as it will curl. I have found that holding the spool at the ends between the thumb and index finger of the right hand and drawing the ribbon out with the left hand, helps to keep it flat.

Ribbon, linen and cotton thread should not be knitted in plain stockinette stitch, because, for some unknown reason, the tension draws the stitches and they form diagonally, not straight up and down. This is why for plain ribbon knitting, one always knits in the back of the knit stitch, unless otherwise stated in the directions.

Remember the ribbon must be held flat so that each stitch comes off the needle uncrushed. The ribbon should always remain in the same position over the index finger, either left or right, whether one knits the Continental or English way. One reason (among others) when first learning to knit, one should not keep throwing the thread over the needle with the hand.

RIBBON STITCHES

Note: Mark one side of the ribbon with a pencil or other identification. This is the side that should be against the needle and the marking will help you to keep it in position. Large needles are used, #8 to #10, and you should obtain anywhere from 4 to 5½ stitches per inch.

TWISTED STOCKINETTE STITCH

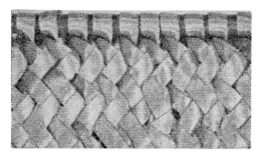

ILLUSTRATION 21.

Knit Side

Step 1: Insert the right-hand needle through the back of the stitch on the left-hand needle. [See Illustration 22.] The dark side is the marked side.

ILLUSTRATION 22.

Step 2: Place the ribbon over the needle from the back to the front, the same as in ordinary knitting, as in Illustration 23.

ILLUSTRATION 23.

Step 3: Pull the loop through then slip the stitch off the left-hand needle. [Illustration 24.] *Note the marked side of the ribbon.*

ILLUSTRATION 24.

Step 4: Continue to the end of the row.

Purl Side

Step 1: Insert the needle from right to left in front of the stitch, as in Illustration 25—like ordinary purling.

ILLUSTRATION 25.

Step 2: Place the ribbon over the needle from the front to the back, as in Illustration 26.

ILLUSTRATION 26.

Step 3: Pull the loop through, then slip the stitch off the left-hand needle, as in Illustration 27.

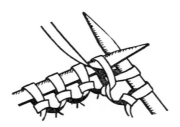

ILLUSTRATION 27.

Step 4: Continue to the end of the row.

WOVEN STITCH

ILLUSTRATION 28.

The difference between the twisted stockinette stitch and the woven stitch is that the yarn is thrown differently both for the knit and the purl.

Knit Side

Step 1: Insert the right-hand needle through the Back of the Stitch on the left-hand needle. [See Illustration 29.]

ILLUSTRATION 29.

Step 2: Place the ribbon over the needle from the front to the back. [See Illustration 30.]

ILLUSTRATION 30.

Step 3: Pull the loop through, then slip the stitch off the left-hand needle, as in Illustration 31.

ILLUSTRATION 31.

Step 4: Continue to the end of the row.

Purl Side

Step 1: Insert the needle from the right to the left in the front of the stitch. [Illustration 32.]

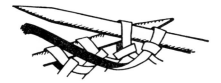

ILLUSTRATION 32.

Step 2: Place the ribbon over the needle from the back to the front, as in Illustration 33.

ILLUSTRATION 33.

Step 3: Pull the loop through, then slip the stitch off the left-hand needle. [See Illustration 34.]

ILLUSTRATION 34.

Step 4: Continue to the end of the row.

Note: If the pattern appears irregular, do not pull the stitch lengthwise. Place the knitting needle or crochet hook under the stitches and pull gently.

YARN AND RIBBON

Often yarn is used with ribbon. Sometimes there are two rows of ribbon and two rows of yarn, which may vary from looped, or nubby, to very fine yarn or thread of wool and rayon, or partly cotton or linen, also metallic threads may be combined. One may also have narrow stripes of yarn and wider ones of ribbon and vice versa.

The following is a good stitch using ribbon and yarn.

RIBBON

Row 1: * K. 1, bring the ribbon to the front, slip a stitch, as if to purl. Take the ribbon to the back * repeat.
Row 2: Purl back.

Yarn or Thread

Row 3: Knit.
Row 4: Purl.
Repeat the four rows.

USING TWO SIZES OF NEEDLES

Occasionally 2 sizes of needles are used, say number 13 and number 4. This gives a long stitch and resembles hairpin lace.

Row 1: Using size 13 needles, knit in the back of the stitch, placing the ribbon over the needle from the back to the front.
Row 2: Using size 4 needles, knit across.

THE STITCH GAUGE FOR RIBBON

The gauge may be from 4 to 5½ stitches to the inch, depending upon the needles (generally size 8 to 10), the type of ribbon, and stitch used. Only 14 to 18 stitches are necessary for a gauge and the ribbon must be steamed and pressed. The stitches should not be stretched, but actually pushed closely together. This is better done with a steam iron, over a light-weight cloth, (organdy is good) on the right side, using the steam and a slight pressure to flatten the stitches. Press a little at a time with the tip of the iron, being careful to use the right temperature for the material.

ADJUSTMENTS FOR WEIGHT OF RIBBON

As skirts made of rayon ribbon have a tendency to be a little weighty, 2 or 3 inches should be allowed for stretch in length, according to the type of skirt and the amount of material used. This is also due to the properties of rayon. It does stretch. Silk is not stretchy, therefore only allow about 1 inch.

Note: Be sure to keep the correct width when measuring.

CHAPTER 37

RIBBON AND MACHINE-KNIT SKIRTS

CHARTING A RIBBON KNIT SKIRT

ALL KNITTED garments should be thought of in terms of sewing, for in order to fit correctly there should be the same principles of clothing-construction involved.

4-GORED RIBBON KNIT SKIRT

Measurements

Waist—28 inches.

Hips—38 inches plus 4 inches for straight skirt = 42 inches, 9 inches down.

Width at the Bottom—hip 42 inches plus 10 inches = 52 inches.

Length of Skirt—30 inches, ½ an inch for 2 rows of crocheting around the bottom, 29½ inches for knitting.

Allowance for Seams—½ inch.

Stitch Gauge—5 stitches to the inch.

Method

4 panels are used, allowing 1 inch extra in width for each gore or panel for seams of ½ inch. See diagrams 61 and 62.

ONE GORE

Bottom—52 inches divided by 4 is 13 inches, plus 1 inch for seams, is 14 inches at the bottom.

Hip—42 inches divided by 4 is 10½ inches, plus 1 inch for seams, is 11½ inches at the hip.

Waist—28 inches divided by 4 is 7 inches, plus 1 inch for seams, is 8 inches at the waist.

KNIT TO FIT

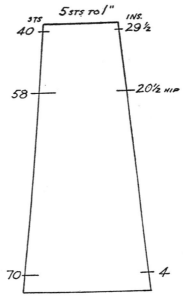

DIAGRAM 61.

ins

last ½ inch even

	29½
8 ins x 5 is 40 sts	29
	28½
	27½
58 sts - 40 is	26½
18 sts. 9 on each	25½
side	24½
	23½
	22½
	21½
11½ ins x 5 is 58 sts	20½ hip
	17½
	14½
70 sts - 58 sts is	11½
12. 6 on each side.	8
	4
14 ins x 5 is 70 sts	

DIAGRAM 62.

MACHINE-KNIT 4-GORED SKIRT

The same diagramming and charting may be used for a 4-gored machine-knit skirt as for the ribbon.

MACHINE-KNIT GORED SKIRTS

Note: 1. A skirt with 4 or more panels or gores, and few stitches to the inch, may be decreased at the sides of each gore, but with a 6, 7 or 8 stitches-to-the-inch gauge, the decreasing should be done across the row, which is a slow process on a machine. However, on a slim skirt, the tension may be changed, using the vital measurement, the hip, to consider the necessary number of stitches.

2. The greater the number of gores, the better fitting the skirt, if decreasing is done at the sides.

3. As it is less confusing to chart without seam allowances, I suggest you do so, then add 4, 6 or 8 stitches to each gore for seams, according to the type of yarn.

MACHINE-KNIT 8-GORED SKIRT

Measurements

Waist—28 inches
Hip—38 inches
Width at Bottom—80 inches
Length—30 inches

Stitch Gauge
7 stitches to the inch
Panels—8

Method

Waist—28 inches × 7 sts. to the inch = 196 sts.

Hip—38 inches plus 2 inches is 40 inches × 7 sts. to the inch = 280 sts.

Width at bottom—80 inches × 7 sts. to the inch = 560 sts.

Total length of skirt is 30 inches minus 1 inch for crochet.

8 panels to be used.

See diagram 63.

In our example, the numbers are divisible by 8, but if they don't divide, take the nearest number divisible by the number of panels to be used.

Waist—196 sts. divided by 8 is 22 sts.
Hip—280 sts. divided by 8 is 35 sts.
Bottom—560 sts. divided by 8 is 70 sts.
Follow the diagram.

Bottom to Waist

70 sts. minus 35 sts. is 35 sts. to be decreased, decreasing on both sides 17 times, and once on one side, making 18 decreases altogether. Therefore, 2 decreases are 2 inches apart and 16 are 1 inch.

Hip to Waist

35 sts. minus 22 sts. are 13 sts. to be decreased, 6 on one side and 7 on the other. 7 decreases in 9 inches, so the first 2 are 2 inches apart and 5 one inch apart.

Note: Don't forget the seam allowances.

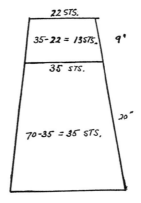

DIAGRAM 63.

PROJECT

1. Diagram and chart a 4-Gored Ribbon or Machine-Knit Skirt with the following:

   Measurements

   > Waist—29 inches.
   > Hips—39 inches plus 4 inches.
   > Width at the Bottom—53 inches.
   > Length of Skirt—31 inches (½-inch crochet allowance).
   > Knitted Length—30½ inches.
   > 1-inch seam allowance for each gore.
   > Stitch Gauge—5 stitches to the inch.

2. Check the answer on pages 272 and 273.

CHAPTER 38

SKIRTS CONTINUED

MEASURING LENGTH

KNITTING MUST be stretched the necessary width before measuring length. The length, too, should be slightly stretched as the material flattens when it is steamed, as you learned when taking a stitch gauge. This applies to yarns made of wool or part-wool. For special novelty yarns, and there are many on the market, use the suggestions offered in the knitting manual for that particular material. We have already considered ribbon and silk. Linen has a tendency to be weighty also, so allow for stretch of 2 or 3 inches depending upon the amount of necessary material.

Note: This doesn't alter the charting of the skirt. Allow for stretch when measuring the length.

FINISHING A RIBBON GORED SKIRT

1. After the blocking of each piece, the seams are basted and sewn, allowing ½-inch seams. This may be done on a machine with a loose fairly long stitch, being sure the rows match at the seams, or by hand with a back stitch. Leave an opening at the left side for a zipper 5 to 7 inches long. Ribbon doesn't stretch like wool or other yarns.

2. Work 2 rows of single-crochet around the lower edge of the skirt and one around the upper, on the right side.

3. Sew in the zipper, leaving ½-inch allowance at the top.

4. Single crochet around the zipper on the right side to hide it.

5. Cut the stiffened belting to the waist measurement, allow-

ing an extra 1½ inches for the turn backs for closing on which the hooks and eyes are fastened.

6. Baste and sew the belting, then the hooks and eyes.

SINGLE CROCHET

ILLUSTRATION 34A.

A Single Crochet is used in knitting for finishing around many types of skirts, to complete the top, and also to flatten the edges of other knitted garments.

Method

Insert the hook into the actual loop of the knit-stitch * thread over the hook and draw the thread through the stitch—2 loops on the hook—thread again over the hook and draw it through both loops * repeat in each stitch.

Note: 1. Use a #1 steel-crochet hook for ribbon, and a number 4 or 5 steel-crochet hook is the best for all general purposes.

2. All single crochet should be made fairly tight when finishing knits. If anything, the edge should be slightly drawn before the garment is steamed.

3. Always crochet on the right side.

CASING

A casing is generally used at the top of a knitted skirt except for ribbon, to hold the elastic. This is worked inside the top of the skirt after several rows of single crochet have been made.

Method

Catch the yarn at the top by means of a slip-stitch, then chain 4, 5 or 6 stitches depending upon the size of the yarn, to make approximately ¾ inch and fasten by means of a slip-stitch with the chain sloping diagonally (as in diagram), first to the top then to the bottom.

DIAGRAM 63A.

LINING RIBBON KNITS

I do not advocate lining a ribbon knit made of rayon or rayon and silk ribbon, if a fairly close pattern stitch has been used. The beauty of all knits is their flexibility. If a tight lining is added, their charm is lost; and they become much too hot and heavy for comfort.

If rayon, silk or nylon ribbons are used in a very loosely knitted, crocheted, or hairpin-lace stitch, they need a foundation. For a slim sheath, a satin foundation may be made the exact size and fastened loosely at the seams by means of catch stitches, or for lighter wear, nylon net or tulle may be used.

You know the measurements of your finished garment, or if you desire, baste and block your garment, then take the pattern from the pieces, allowing ½-inch seams.

Sew the seams, catch stitch them to the garment, then hem around the neckline, bottom and zipper.

I reiterate, one must know dress design to become an expert knit designer.

BLOCKING SKIRTS

In *Chapter 18*, we discussed blocking a sweater and stated the necessary equipment.

Finishing and blocking are the final steps and most important in obtaining a beautiful knit-garment, also it is possible to partially correct some poorly knitted items.

The word *blocking*, to many, is some sort of magic trick that only a few are capable of performing. Actually, it means, pinning, steaming to shape, and flattening where necessary, a knitted or crocheted garment according to the necessary measurements of the individual, and, as I stated in *Chapter 18*, I definitely do not agree that every piece should be blocked separately, except ribbon knits, then in most instances professionals do the finishing and blocking. I have seen some sad shapes with armholes and necklines pulled, steamed, and overpressed way out of line. If the pieces are fastened together, one holds the other in shape.

MEASUREMENTS

Use the measurements that were taken for the finished garment according to the necessary specifications. For ribbon knits where each piece is blocked separately, you know what each should measure; or if knitting from directions from a knitting manual, break down the number of stitches to inches.

1. RIBBON KNITS—each gore separately

Turn to *Chapter 18* for necessary materials.

Note: The big difference between blocking ribbon from other materials is that ribbon garments are placed on the blocking board right side up so you can see that the ribbon is flattened

on the right side. We shall block the panel which was diagrammed on page 160.

Note: We first mark the position for the gore or panel on the
blocking pad.

Method—A

1. Mark the center of the panel, AB, on the board, using
    a long wooden rule.
2. Mark a line CD, at right angles to AB, where the waist
    of the panel is to be pinned, using ½ the waist measure-
    ment on each side, which is 4 inches.
3. Measure 9 inches down AB, and mark EF, at right
    angles to it, using ½ the hip (for each panel) on each
    side, which is 5¾ inches.
4. On AB, measure 29½ inches which is the length of the
    finished skirt—29½ inches before crocheting. The other
    ½ inch is added when the skirt panels are put together.
5. Draw GH at right angles to AB, using ½ the width at
    the bottom of the panel, which is 7 inches on each side.

Method—B

1. With pins, mark the center of the actual panel on the
    right side.
2. Pin the center of the panel to center AB.
3. Pin the waist to CD.
4. Pin bottom to GH.
5. Pin hip to EF.
6. Pull the sides and pin in place, pins about 1 inch apart
    (use rule to be sure the edges are straight).
7. Press each panel as stated for ribbon stitch gauge.
8. Leave on the pad until dry.
9. Press pin marks down the center.
10. Block each panel separately.
11. Complete the skirt as in *Chapter 37*.
12. Press the seams and check the measurements.

Note: For skirts which are made partly of ribbon, e.g. ribbon stripes, and using a circular needle, I would advise that the

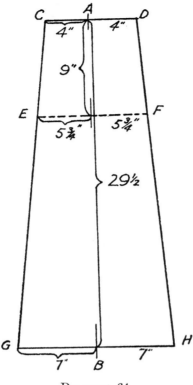

DIAGRAM 64.

ribbon stripes are partly pressed before being blocked like a yarn skirt, the directions for which follow.

2. BLOCKING SKIRTS MADE ON A CIRCULAR NEEDLE

The principle for pinning skirts made on a circular needle is very much the same as blocking a panel, except that skirts knitted of materials other than ribbon, are all turned on the wrong side to block and are completely finished before any steaming takes place.

For a dress, it is better to block the skirt and top separately if possible. At any rate, the skirt should be completed, i.e., the casing for the elastic worked or the belting sewn in.

We shall take for our example, the measurements of the skirt diagrammed in *Chapter 29*.

Remember, we block to the finished measurements.

Waist—28 inches.

Hip—42 inches (9 inches down).

Width at the bottom—52 inches.

Length—30 inches.

Follow diagram 65 and mark the measurements on the blocking pad, the same as for the panel.

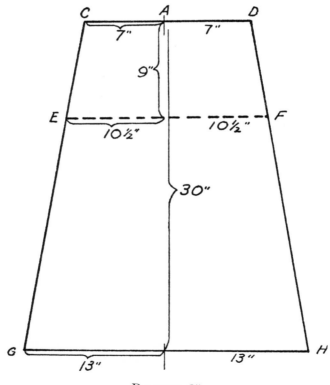

DIAGRAM 65.

Method

1. Place the pins down the center front and the center back of the skirt, dividing it in two.
2. ½ the waist, 28 inches is 14 inches, therefore, 7 inches on each side of the center.
3. ½ of the finished hip, 42 inches, is 21 inches, therefore, 10½ inches on each side of center front (9 inches down).
4. ½ of the width at the bottom, 52 inches, is 26 inches, 13 inches each side of the center.
5. Pin the center front and the center back together down the center line, AB.
6. Complete the pinning as for the panel.
7. Steam as for the sweater, *Chapter 18*, #14 to #17.

PROJECT

Test your ability on a skirt.

CHAPTER 40

FITTED JACKETS

WE HAVE diagrammed and charted basic, simple upper garments, with normal shoulders, normal armscyes with only the fullness added that gives the necessary amount of ease. Now we consider fitted jackets that are large enough to be worn over sweaters, blouses, etc.

MEASUREMENTS

Differences in:

(a) Waist

It is advisable not to knit the waist too tight, therefore, a slight surplus width is necessary. However, the amount really depends upon individual needs. A poor figure should never wear a too tight-fitting garment.

Generally 2 inches for the entire waist is allowed, that is, 1 inch more for the back measurement and 1 inch for the front.

(b) Bust

For fitted jackets, no matter what the type of figure, a difference is made between the width of the front and the back.

Use the across the back measurement from underarm seam to underarm seam and the front bust measurement from underarm seam to underarm seam, then add 2 inches to the total measurement, that is, 1 inch to the back and 1 inch to the front. More may be added if the figure calls for it. Remember that a large woman with a good figure looks well in fitted clothes and if too much is added, she appears to be larger.

(c) Armhole or Armscye

1 inch is added to the total armscye measurement, as taken in *Chapter 3*, that is, ½ inch to each ½ armhole measurement.

Note: All the measurements to be taken as explained in *Chapter 3*, then the necessary amounts added.

172

(d) The underarm to waist measurement

The underarm to waist measurement is ½ inch shorter than the basic sweater measurement, therefore, after measuring fom the waist to the armpit, as explained in *Chapter 3*, 1½ inches are deducted, not 1 inch, as for the sweater.

(e) Shoulder to shoulder measurement

The shoulders for jackets are a little longer so an extra garment may be worn underneath.

Allow ½ inch more on each side of the tip of the shoulder, that is, 1 inch more than the measurement which was taken from the tip to the tip.

(f) Sleeve underarm length

The sleeve underarm length is ½ inch shorter because of the larger armscye, therefore, 1½ inches are deducted from the wrist to the armpit measurement, not 1 inch as in the case of sweaters.

(g) Length of jacket

This depends entirely upon the figure, as did the length of the cardigan.

Example of Changes

SWEATER	JACKET
Waist—26 inches	26 inches + 2 is 28 inches
Across the Back—18 inches	18 inches + 1 is 19 inches
Front Bust—19 inches	19 inches + 1 is 20 inches
Underarm to Waist—8 inches	8 inches − ½ inch is 7½ inches
Shoulder to Shoulder— 14½ inches	14½ inches + 1 inch is 15½ inches
Sleeve Underarm Length— 18 inches	18 inches − ½ inch is 17½ inches
Wrist—6 inches	6 inches
Upperarm—11 inches	11 inches
Armscye—18 inches	18 inches + 1 inch is 19 inches

PROJECT

1. With woman's measurements as in *Chapter 6,* and the across the back underarm—17½ inches, the front bust measurement—18½ inches, state the difference in measurements for a jacket from a basic sweater.

2. Check answers on page 274.

CHAPTER 41

FITTED JACKETS—CONTINUED

DARTS

DARTS, whether used in sewing or knitting, are to add or take out width in order that the garment may curve where necessary. The aim of a well-fitting garment is to make it appear as though it has been molded to the figure.

Yes, it is possible to make darts when knitting. The surplus width is taken out by decreasing, and extra width is added by increasing at the correct places.

VERTICAL WAIST DARTS

Vertical darts are knitted at right angles to the waist and hip lines and give form to the garments. They should be knitted on a line with the shoulder blades at the back and with the bust in front. The height and depth of the dart varies with the individual.

Note: In a fitted jacket, if all the stitches were decreased or increased at the sides, points would be formed at the underarm seams and blocking would not alter the effect.

SHOULDER DARTS

The purpose of the shoulder dart is to eliminate some of the surplus width that was necessary for the curve of the bust. In inexpensive clothes, a larger amount is taken out at the armhole, but this gives a very poor fit.

175

The shoulder dart is generally placed in the center of the shoulder and tapers gradually toward the fullest point of the bust.

Measurements

    Half the Waist—15 inches
    The back underarm measurement—20 inches
    The front bust measurement—22 inches
    Underarm to waist—8 inches
    Hips (5 inches down)—35 inches
    Waist to bottom—5 inches
       Stitch gauge—8 stitches to the inch

Note: In a fitted jacket, where the shoulder measurement is 1 inch longer, the extra stitches are not used for the back of the neck.

BACK

Method

1. Bottom to waist, see diagram 66.
2. Half the waist is 15 inches times 8 stitches to the inch = 120 stitches.
3. The across the back measurement is 20 inches times 8 stitches to the inch = 160 stitches.
4. The difference between 160 stitches and 120 stitches is 40 stitches to increase from the waist to the underarm. Divide by 4, which is 10 stitches to increase at each side and 10 stitches to add at 2 vertical waist darts.
5. Increase 10 stitches in each dart, 2 stitches at a time, every 1½ inches and 10 stitches at each side, every ¾ inch.

Note: 1. The vertical dart is placed about ¼ of the distance of the waist measurement.
    2. Place a marker at this point, then the dart is made by increasing in a stitch, K. 1, before the marker, then K. 1 and

increasing a stitch after the marker, i.e., knit 28 stitches, increase in a stitch, K. 1 marker, K. 1 increase in a stitch.

6. Follow the diagram—no shoulder dart is necessary.

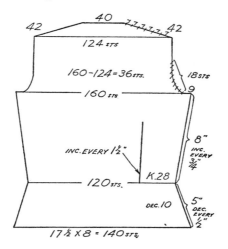

DIAGRAM 66.

FRONT

1. Across the front bust—22 inches. Half is 11 inches, times 8 stitches to the inch = 88 stitches, so both the front and back side shaping is the same. Increase 10 stitches at the side, allowing 18 stitches to be increased in a dart.

2. Place the marker at half the waist measurement, 30 stitches, then increase before and after the marker 9 times, every ¾ inch, at the same time increasing at the side, 10 times.

3. Shoulder dart

As there are 8 extra stitches at the front, these 8 stitches must be decreased in a dart toward the center of the shoulder. Place a marker after the 25th stitch and decrease instead of increasing every inch, 4 times.

ILLUSTRATION 35.

Note: 1. 21 stitches is the center of the shoulder, but 4 stitches have to be added to allow for decreasing at one side of the dart making 25 stitches. See diagram 67.

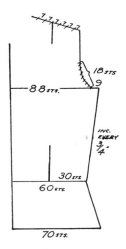

DIAGRAM 67.

2. If a line were drawn, the vertical dart would meet the shoulder dart.

PROJECT

1. Diagram and chart the back and front of a fitted jacket using the same measurements as the example, but with 7 sts. to the inch.

2. Check answers on pages 274 and 275.

Chapter 42

RAGLANS

KNIT-IN RAGLANS FOR SWEATER, COAT OR CAPE

Using a circular needle ,we begin a knit-in raglan at the neck, working the back, sleeves and front altogether, and continue knitting until the underarm seams are reached for sweaters and coats, and to the tips of the shoulders for capes. See illustration 36.

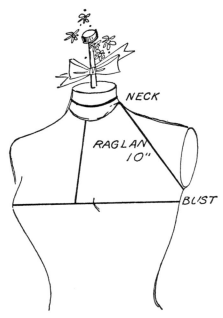

Illustration 36.

Note: 1. A 14-inch neckline is the one chosen first because it is the size which is perfect for figuring.

2. The type of neckline is not considered at this point, but the number of stitches required for the increases, the back, the front and the sleeves.

Measurements

Neck—14 inches   Stitch Gauge—6 stitches to the inch
Raglan—10 inches   8 rows to the inch

Method

14 inches multiplied by 6 stitches to the inch = 84 stitches for the total neckline.

Note: If we are going to have an opening in the front and a turned-back lapel, all the stitches are cast on at one time, but when a shaped neckline is desired, the front has to be shaped gradually the same as for a sweater with set-in sleeves.

PROPORTIONING THE STITCHES

1. 8 stitches are needed for the increases.
2. 5 inches of stitches are allowed for the back of the neck. 5 multiplied by 6 stitches to the inch is 30 stitches.
3. 1 inch or 6 stitches is allotted for each sleeve, therefore 12 stitches for 2.

We have, therefore, 8 stitches for the increases, 30 stitches for the back of the neck, 12 stitches for the sleeves, making **50** stitches. 50 stitches from the total of 84 stitches leaves 34 stitches, 17 stitches for each front.

Note: As it is easier to understand when all the stitches are cast on at the beginning, this method is explained first.

Method

1. Using a circular needle, cast on 84 stitches, but do not join. Purl back, so it is easier to increase in the necessary stitches.

2. Follow diagram 68. Knit 17 sts. for the front, increase
in the next stitch, place a marker on the needle, increase
in the next stitch, knit 6 sts. Sleeve, increase in the next
stitch, place a marker, increase in the next stitch, knit
30 sts. Back of the neck, increase in the next stitch, place
a marker, increase in the next stitch, knit 6 sts. for the
other sleeve, increase in the next stitch, place a marker,
increase in the next stitch, knit 17 sts. for the front.

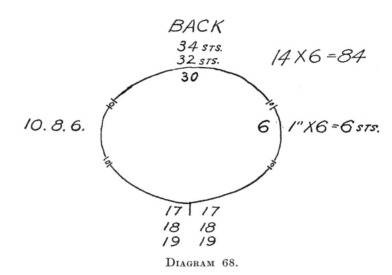

DIAGRAM 68.

Each of the increases made a new stitch, so there are
now 84 plus 8 stitches which = 92 stitches.
3. As there is an opening in the front, the second row is
purled (no increases), passing the markers from one
needle to another.
4. For a slipover sweater, the work is joined and every second round knitted without any increases. However, the
number of stitches at the neckline must be increased,
allowing 1 extra inch of sts. for the back of the neck, and

1 inch extra for the front, for a high round neck or turtle-necked sweater.

5. Continue increasing before and after the markers, every second row or round, until the raglan measures 10 inches or the necessary bust or chest measurement has been reached.

Note: Before placing the sleeve stitches on another needle, test the measurements by adding 1½ inches of sts. to the back sts. and 1½ inches to the front. Add these together and multiply by the stitch gauge to see if the chest measurement has been reached.

6. Leave all the stitches, except for one sleeve, on the circular needle. With a straight needle, add ¾ inch of sts.; 4 in this case, to each side of the sleeves, as well as to the back and fronts, when we come to them.
7. Work the sleeve back and forth, reversing the shape as for a sweater with set-in sleeves.
8. Work the other sleeve.
9. Add the underarm sts. to the fronts and back—these may be worked separately or all in one.
10. Complete, in reverse, as for sweater with set-in sleeves.

RAGLAN WITH OVAL NECKLINE

Follow diagrams 69 and 70.

There were 34 sts. allotted for the front of the neck. 2 of these are cast on with the stitches for the sleeves, and the back of the neck, making 52 sts., leaving 32 sts. to be added for the neck shaping, 16 sts. for each side.

Work as previously, but increase both fronts, every other row, 1 stitch, at the neck edge, 12 times, then cast on 4 sts. each side.

When all the front stitches have been added, join the work and knit round and round.

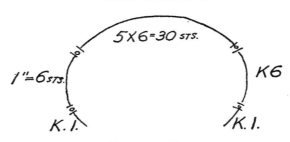

DIAGRAM 69.

32 STS FOR FRONT

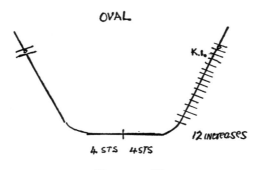

DIAGRAM 70.

PROJECT

Start sample raglans, using the same measurement and stitch gauge.

    a.   All the stitches at one time.

    b.   With "V" neckline.

Chapter 43

RAGLANS WITH DIFFERENT STITCH GAUGES OR SIZE OF NECKLINES

1.   15-inch neckline and 6 sts. to the inch. [See diagram 71. It is self-explanatory.]

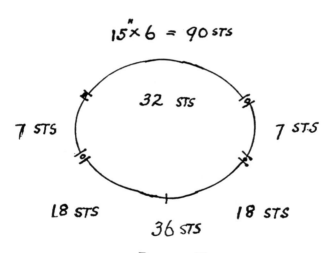

DIAGRAM 71.

2.   16-inch neckline and 7 sts. to the inch. Diagram 72 is almost self-explanatory.

16 inches multiplied by 7 sts. to the inch is 112 sts. Proportioning the stitches from the 14-inch neckline, we require 40 sts. for the back of the neck, 9 sts. for each sleeve, and 8 sts. for the increasing, making 66 sts. and 46 sts. for the total front.

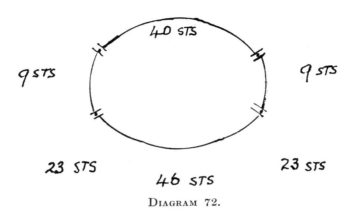

$$16'' \times 7 = 112 \text{ STS}$$

40 STS

9 STS   9 STS

23 STS   23 STS

46 STS

DIAGRAM 72.

RAGLANS WITH SET-IN SLEEVES
These may be worked on a machine.

Method

Diagram and chart the sweater the same as a sweater with set-in sleeves to the armholes, back, front and sleeves.

BACK

Bind off ¾ inch of sts. on both sides, then knit 2 together at the beginning and end of every front row, until the raglan measurement is reached, and approximately 5 inches of sts. remain. See diagram 73.

FRONT

The front is knitted the same as the back until the neckline is reached.

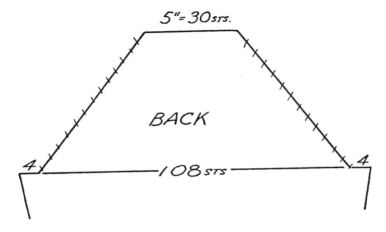

$5'' = 30$ STS.

BACK

4

4

108 STS

DIAGRAM 73.

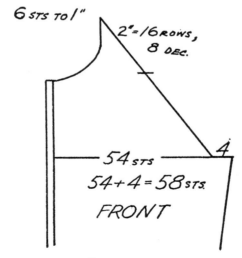

6 STS TO 1"

$2'' = 16$ ROWS, 8 DEC.

4

54 STS

$54 + 4 = 58$ STS.

FRONT

DIAGRAM 74.

Method

    a. Using the back, count the number of sts. still to be decreased in the raglan from where the neckline is begun.

    b. Subtract these from the total number of sts. to know how many to take off at the neck edge.

    c. Figure the neck sts. the same as a sweater with set-in sleeves and complete the raglan.

SLEEVES

The raglan must be the same length as the back raglan.

    a. Work the sleeve to the underarm.

    b. Bind off ¾ inch of sts. on both sides.

    c. Knit 2 together at the beginning and end of the front rows until the desired length of raglan is reached.

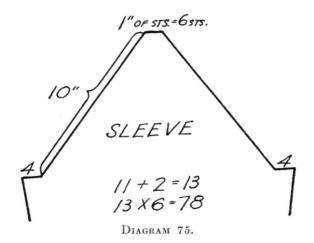

DIAGRAM 75.

PROJECT

Diagram the back and left front of a raglan with set-in sleeves, with a high, round neckline, using the same measurements as in *Chapter 6*, and 7 sts. to the inch.

See answers on pages 278 and 279.

CHAPTER 44

MISCELLANEOUS

CAPES

A WELL-FITTING cape should lie flat across the shoulders, therefore, increase as for raglans, until the tip of the shoulder is reached, approximately 5 to $5\frac{1}{2}$ inches. The seam will show across the shoulders where the 8 increases were made. Now the 8 increases may be spread out, or, if extra fullness is desired at the back or all around, extra increases may be added, evenly distributed where the folds should fall and the increases made on the right side of the work.

DOLMAN, BAT OR WINGED SLEEVES

All these names apply to the same type of sleeve, a wider sleeve which resembles the wing of a bat.

Armhole or Armscye for Dolman Sleeve

The only difference between the armhole of a dolman sleeve and a normal armhole is that it is deeper. For a normal set-in sleeve, we require a 17 or 18-inch armhole. A dolman sleeve has, at least, a 2-inch deeper armhole, which requires the following changes in the garment.

Normal Sleeve	*Dolman Sleeve*
Upperarm—10 inches	
Armhole—18 inches, $\frac{1}{2}$, 9 inches	9 inches $+$ 2 inches is 11 inches
Cap of Sleeve—$5\frac{1}{2}$ inches deep	$5\frac{1}{2}$ inches $+$ 2 inches is $7\frac{1}{2}$ inches

189

Normal Sleeve

Underarm to Waist—8 inches

Sleeve Underarm Length—
   18 inches

Dolman Sleeve

8 inches — 2 inches is
   6 inches

18 inches — 2 inches is
   16 inches

A LONG, DOLMAN SLEEVE

This is a long dolman sleeve made at the same time as the body of the garment with a seam at the center sleeve and shoulder.

Measurements

1. The underarm to waist measurement—8 inches minus 3 inches leaves 5 inches.
2. The underarm sleeve measurement is 18 inches minus 3 inches leaves 15 inches.
3. Width at the wrist is 8 inches, half is 4 inches.
   Stitch Gauge—8 stitches to the inch.

Method

Follow diagram 76.
1. For the curve at the underarm, add 1 stitch every other row for 1 inch, or 8 times, then add 4 stitches every other row, 4 times, making the 3 inch sleeve curve.
2. 15 inches times 8 stitches to the inch = 120 stitches, to be added all at once.
3. Knit even for 4 inches or the desired width for half the wrist measurement.
4. Bind off 4 stitches, which is half an inch of stitches, every other row, until 60 stitches have been bound off, half the length of the sleeve.
5. Bind off 1 inch of stitches until the shoulder stitches remain.
6. Bind off the shoulder stitches.

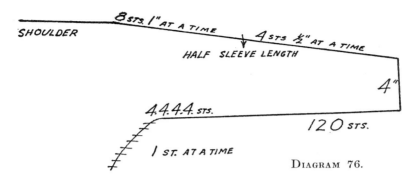

DIAGRAM 76.

Method for Long Dolman Sleeve

1. Curve at the Underarm.
    Add 1 stitch, every other row for 1 inch of stitches, then half an inch of stitches, every other row, until the length of the sleeve curve has been added.
2. Add the total number of stitches for the desired length of the sleeve.
3. Knit even for the desired width of the sleeve at the wrist. (Half the wrist measurement)
4. For sleeves of an average width, bind off half an inch of stitches, until half the length of the sleeve has been reached, then 1 inch of stitches until the shoulder line is reached.
5. Bind off the shoulder stitches.

Note: a. The binding off at the center seam depends upon the desired width.

b. If no seam is desired at the center of the sleeve, reverse the shaping.

PROJECTS

1. State the necessary changes in measurements when using a dolman sleeve.
2. Using the same measurements as the example, and 6 stitches to the inch, diagram and chart a long, dolman sleeve.
3. Check the answers on pages 279 and 280.

CHAPTER 45

SHORTIE COATS

EVERY VACATION wardrobe requires a Shortie Coat. As figure, taste and purse vary, so does the type which one conjures up in her mind. However, all must have the important qualities of design and good workmanship.

As short coats are very often carried, they must not be heavy or cumbersome and fashioned so that they are appropriate from early morning until the wee hours of night. Yes, such a coat is possible, and especially if it is hand knitted, then, there's no trouble about fuss or muss and it is ready at any hour of the day, whether it has reclined on a luggage rack, in a drawer or been slung over one's arm.

There are many types of shortie coats.

1. Squared box-jacket, cropped short just below the waist—no sticking out derrières for this length—make the coat longer if the figure isn't too good.

2. Hip-length coats with three-quarter wide sleeves.

3. Short coats with a gentle flare or wider ones if desired.

4. Raglan sleeved coats, hip-length or longer to suit individual needs.

Note: I want to emphasize one thing particularly. No wide short coat should ever be worn with a very full skirt, no matter what type of figure. It takes away from the slimness of a pretty silhouette and adds considerable weight to the large person. Too-wide shoulders aren't good either. For all purposes, the extra inch for shoulders as for jackets is all that is needed. Women should look feminine at all times.

The same applies to capes; however, in a short cape, there is a break in the silhouette, where a slim waist breaks the lines.

ILLUSTRATION 37.

1. SQUARED BOX-JACKET

Without any added instructions, you should almost be able to diagram this type.

BACK

Method

A box coat generally has straight lines, so the width at the bottom is the same as the across-the-back-underarm measurement. 2 inches is generally sufficient to add to the across-the-back-underarm measurement that was taken in *Chapter 5* for sweaters. More may be added if a roomier coat is desired. Test the width at the bottom.

Measurements as in Chapter 41

Across-the-back-underarm—18 inches plus 2 inches = 20 inches.

Front bust—20 inches plus 2 inches = 22 inches.

Armscye—18 inches plus 2 inches = 20 inches, more if desired.

Shoulder-to-shoulder—14½ inches plus 1 inch = 15½ inches.

Length of coat from the underarm—10 to 14 inches.

Stitch Gauge—7 stitches to the inch.

BACK

Follow diagram 77. It is self-explanatory.

FRONT

The coat has a high, round neckline, so 6 extra stitches are added to each front for an overlap of 12 stitches for buttons and buttonholes.

Note: The extra 8 stitches for each front are reduced by means of a shoulder dart as in *Chapter 41*.

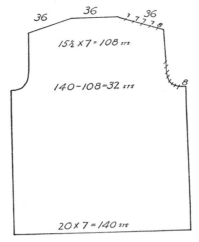

DIAGRAM 77.

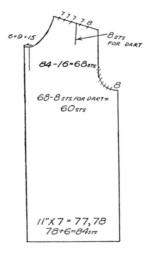

DIAGRAM 77A.

SLEEVE (this is a coat sleeve)

Width at the bottom—12 inches.
Width at the upperarm—16 inches.
Length—17 inches.
Cap—6½ inches deep or more.
Diagram 78 is self-explanatory.

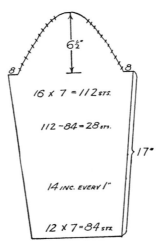

DIAGRAM 78.

PROJECT

1. Diagram and chart a Box Coat.

    Measurements
    Across the back underarm—22 inches.
    6 stitches allowed for the overlap in front.
    The front bust measurement—24 inches.
    Sleeve—¾ sleeve, 14 inches long, 13 inches at the bottom, widening to 15 inches.
    The other measurements the same as the example.
    Stitch gauge—7 stitches to the inch.

2. Check answers on pages 280 to 283.

2. HIP LENGTH COAT WITH WIDE, 3/4 SLEEVES—SLIGHT FULLNESS AT THE BACK AND FITTED FROM THE UNDERARM

Measurements

Width at the bottom—back—29 inches.
Width at the bottom—front—25 inches.
Length from the underarm—16 inches.
Armhole—21 inches.
Sleeve—14 inches long, shaped from 13 inches to 16 inches.

Method

It is always better to chart the back first, because the sides of the back and front must be shaped the same, also the shoulders must fit, making darts at the front shoulders necessary. Follow diagrams 79 and 80.

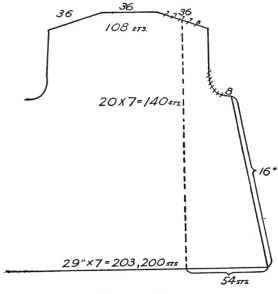

DIAGRAM 79.

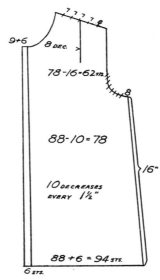

DIAGRAM 80.

BACK

Width at the bottom—29 inches times 7 stitches to the inch = 203 stitches, 200 stitches for even 10s.

Across-the-back-underarm—20 inches times 7 stitches to the inch = 140 stitches.

200 stitches minus 140 stitches leaves 60 stitches to decrease to the armscye.

The length of the coat to the underarm seam is 16 inches. Allowing for 2 flares as well as decreasing at the sides, 6 into 60 makes 10 decreases, every 1½ inches at the sides, and 20 stitches to decrease in each flare, making 40 stitches—60 stitches altogether.

POSITION OF THE FLARES

The center of the shoulder is 18 stitches, plus 16 stitches to take off for the armhole, plus 10 stitches to decrease at the underarm seam, plus 10 stitches to decrease for half a flare, makes a total of 54 stitches. Therefore, place 2 markers, marking the position of the 2 flares, which are 54 stitches from each end.

Note: This is the nearest position of the flares; more stitches may be added if the fullness is desired toward the back.

FLARES

For darts, only 1 stitch was allotted before and after the marker. Here, it is better to leave 6 stitches, so the flare will have a better shape. The first decrease at 1½ inches will be: knit to within 8 stitches of the marker, then knit 2 together, knit 6 stitches, move the marker, knit 6 stitches, then knit 2 together. The same for the other flare, decreasing 2 stitches each time, every 1½ inches, the same as the sides.

Note: For a very wide back, it could be decreased the same as a full skirt, decreasing 10 or 20 stitches at a time.

FRONT

The front is diagrammed the same as the box coat (described earlier in this Chapter) except the side seams are decreased the same as the back.

SLEEVE

The sleeve is self-explanatory. (See diagram 81, next page.)

3. SHORT COAT WITH GREATER WIDTH AT THE BACK

BACK—THREE FLARES

Measurements

Width at the bottom—37 inches
Underarm seam—18 inches
Armscye—22 inches
Remainder—the same measurements as #2
Stitch gauge—7 sts. to the inch

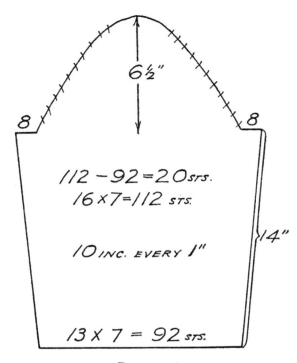

112 − 92 = 20 sts.

16 × 7 = 112 sts.

10 inc. every 1"

13 × 7 = 92 sts.

DIAGRAM 81.

POSITION OF FLARES

1. The front is the same as diagram 79, so the decreasing at the side seams is 12 decreases every 1½ inches.

Note: On this type of coat, the flares do not stop at the under-arm, but continue to about 5 inches below the tip of the shoulder. If they continued all the way, the shoulders would droop.

2. The center of the shoulder is 18 stitches, plus 16 stitches to take off for the armscye, plus 16 stitches to decrease for one half flare, plus 12 stitches to decrease at the side seam, making a total of 62 stitches.

3. As there are 3 flares, see diagram 82, and 4 spaces; 4 into 260 stitches goes 65 times, approximately 62 stitches, therefore, place the markers at every 65th stitch, and decrease every 1½ inches, as for previous coat.

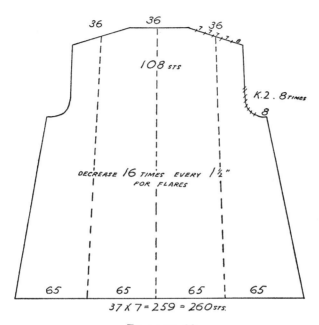

36   *36*   *36*

108 sts

K.2 . 8 times

8

DECREASE *16* TIMES EVERY *1½"*
FOR FLARES

65   *65*   *65*   *65*

37 X 7 = 259 = 260 sts.

DIAGRAM 82.

3. RAGLANS

Consider the top of a raglan-sleeved short coat in the same light as a raglan sweater with set-in sleeves, knitting the back first, then the fronts, and finally the sleeves, the same as the directions for the previous shortie coat. Complete the raglans as for raglans with set-in sleeves, *Chapter 43*.

PROJECT

Spend considerable time, absorbing the mathematics used in shortie coats.

Chapter 46

BLOCKING JACKETS AND SHORT COATS

MADE OF RIBBON

BLOCK EACH piece made of ribbon separately, according to the measurements, before sewing them together, then flatten the seams. Be very careful not to stretch the armscye, neckline, etc. Turn to *Chapters 36* and *37* to refresh your memory.

It is easier to steam or block garments made of other materials, e.g., yarn, cotton, wool-yarn-and-cotton, linen yarns and metallics, when they are crocheted together.

JACKETS

Turn to *Chapter 18*. The same principles apply to blocking jackets as blocking sweaters, with the exception of the side seams and the two fronts, so follow the same directions to #9, adding at #5, the waist-to-the-bottom-of-the-jacket-measurement, also across the hip measurement (of the jacket) and pin into position.

Note: Don't forget to use the measurements for the jacket which differ from the sweater measurements.

10. Pin down one center front, allowing for extra width and overlap.

11. Adjust half the neckline and pin in position.

12. Pin down the other center front, allowing for extra width and overlap.

13. Adjust the other half neckline.

Continue #12 to #17.

SHORTIE COATS

We have knitted to the measurement of the finished garment, so the blocking is easy and there is absolutely no guesswork as there is when following measurements of supposed size 32, 34, etc.

The garments have the shape and correct size desired and there is no possibility of having to overstretch for fit. Now you realize why the stitch gauge and taking measurements are very important.

Shortie coats are blocked in the same manner as jackets, but it is possible that blocking—in the sense of pinning to the board —isn't necessary, just steam flat with a steam iron.

LINING A SHORT COAT

It may be that one would like a lined jacket. Of course, we have no actual paper pattern. We have our measurements, however; but for the layman I would suggest you baste the coat with fairly close basting stitches, then steam or block it. Pull out the basting threads and use the pieces for a paper pattern, allowing ⅜-inch seams. In this way the fit of the lining is assured.

CUFFS ON A SHORT COAT

If one would like cuffs on the bottom of the sleeves, ½ inch more stitches should be allowed at the beginning [make separately]—then increase at both sides, every other row, or every 4th row, according to desired increase—make the cuffs as wide as desired, 3, 4, or 5 inches.

Note: The joining of the cuff isn't sewn to the center of the wrist, but a little more toward the back, on a line with the elbow, actually ⅓ of the remaining ½.

COLLAR

The same applies to a large stand-up collar, but this time, pick up the stitches instead of sewing on afterwards, as in the case of the cuffs.

PROJECT

Now you are ready to block anything. Test your ability.

FACINGS

I have found that knitted facings are often too bulky. For all general purposes, I suggest grosgrain ribbon, which has a picot edge, and makes handling easier. The ribbon should be shrunk before using, either with a damp cloth and warm iron, or a steam iron.

As I suggested for sweaters, the garment should be first steamed to flatten the material, then the measurement taken for the facing either on the person or a dress-form, allowing 1 inch extra for turn-ins.

For jackets and coats where wide facings are necessary for the collar, lapels, and down the fronts, any lining material that a dressmaker usually uses is all right. The pieces for the collar and the lapels should be slightly smaller to allow for the turn-down or roll, and all pieces should be cut straight on the grain of the material.

Note: Before cutting the material smaller, test around the hand for the desired roll.

Catch-stitch in a zig-zag manner, both the lining for the collar and the lapels.

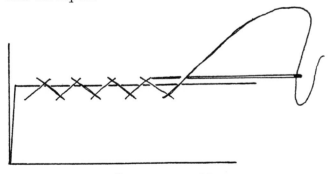

ILLUSTRATION 38.

STRENGTHENING THE SHOULDER LINE

Seam binding may be sewn to the shoulder seams and across the back of the neck to prevent sagging.

CHAPTER 47

CHILDREN'S KNITTED WEAR

As AGE IS the poorest predictor of children's body measurements—for many children of the same age have entirely different body proportions—we are fortunate that we have mastered the taking of measurements for all sizes and are able to adjust the measurements to suit the style, material, and need of the child.

I do want to offer a word of caution, however; do not add an inch here and an inch there to allow for growth. Let us consider an upperarm measurement of $9\frac{1}{2}$ inches which was made $10\frac{1}{2}$ inches, then 2 inches more added for the width of a sleeve as for an adult, instead of the necessary $1\frac{1}{2}$ inches for a child. This was large enough for a medium-sized woman.

There are three essentials for children's garments:

1. Ease in dressing—simple design.
2. Large enough to take into consideration rapid growth.
3. Suitable color.

As we know how to lengthen and shorten all necessary parts, let us make them correctly in the first place and have a happy, contented comfortable child.

Note: It isn't necessary to decrease at the hips of a skirt for a child. Decrease straight from the bottom to the waist.

For sizes 1, 2, 3 and 4, I think it advisable to add all the necessary stitches for the width of a sleeve on the first row after the ribbing. A fitted sleeve isn't always practical unless one is making a small coat sleeve, then don't make that too fitted.

On the next page is a chart of measurements which might be valuable to those who instruct in knit shops, designers, or those who wish to make sweaters, etc., of a specific size.

These measurements are the finished measurements after the article has been steamed or blacked.

Sizes	2	3	4	6	8	10	12	14
Chest	23	24	25	26½	28	29½	31	33
Underarm to Waist (includes rib.)	8	9	10	10½	11	11½	12½	13
Upperarm	9	10	10½	11	11	11½	12	12½
Armhole (around)	10	10½	11	12	13	14	15	16
Underarm Sleeve	8	9	10	11	12	13	14½	16
Shoulder-to-Shoulder	10½	11	11½	12	12½	13	13½	14

PROJECTS

1. Diagram and chart the following skirts:

    (a) Plain—stockinette
        Waist—24 inches
        Length—19 inches
        Width—48 inches
        Stitch Gauge—6 stitches to the inch
    (b) Pleated—same measurements as above
        Bottom—52 inches
        Pleats—3 inches wide

2. Check measurements on pages 283 to 285.

CHAPTER 48

OPERATING A KNIT SHOP

NECESSARY QUALIFICATIONS FOR SUCCESS

"I'VE BEEN KNITTING since I was six. Many have asked me to teach them to knit, so I think I'll open a Knit Shop."

How little is understood of the attributes necessary to operate a successful business!

Knitting has developed into High Fashion (apart from knitting mittens, socks, hats, etc.) and entails a knowledge of knit design, and color, as well as merchandising, advertising, understanding of personality traits and a knowledge of business acumen, which can only be gained through learning, understanding and experience.

1. SKILL

Skill in giving instructions and directions to the customer. This doesn't mean that one should be able to knit and purl adequately or even be able to follow instructions from a knitting manual, but one must have a thorough knowledge of knit design, and be able to change any instruction to suit individual needs and wants, as well as be able to diagram and chart every possible garment for any type of figure, ranging from sweaters to evening gowns. This, of course, entails every skill, including finishing, blocking and lining, if necessary.

2. KNOWLEDGE OF MERCHANDISE

One of the most difficult materials to know in the U.S.A. and Canada are the different yarns, threads, ribbons, etc., from which knitted garments are made. We have already spoken of some of the more common yarns, but there are literally hundreds of different types and brands sold by different distributors and manufacturers, and from many countries of the world. My suggestion is to spend as much time as possible in large Art Needlework Departments—different stores will carry different brands because of their franchises—or better still, become proficient in diagramming and charting, and gain experience as an instructor. There is no better way of learning the potentialities of different yarns.

One must know how to buy yarn and needles intelligently. An adequate stock of each should be kept on hand, and I suggest some no-dye-lot yarns for general use, especially for beginners. Do not be afraid to stock a staple brand because a large department store carries the same. Your personality and courtesy to customers will soon overcome the difference in size, for this is one business where automation cannot take over. It is important, also, to know the correct amount of yarn to sell to a customer for her requirements. It is impossible to state here the amounts, for there are so many yarns, but my suggestion is to refer to the knitting manual which is using that brand, for a similar type of garment. And lastly, be careful not to undersell yarns with a dye number.

3. KNOWLEDGE OF FASHION TRENDS

Knits are the closest to four-season apparel, and wearable any time of day. They also pack well, travel well, and shed wrinkles. This emphasizes the fact that one must keep up with fashion trends.

I suggest you subscribe to and digest the material in the leading women's magazines, *Harpers Bazaar, Vogue, Glamor, Seventeen,* etc. It isn't simply knits from which one garners inspirations! One learns good styling in a subtle way. Note color trends, but do not become an addict to fashionable colors. The important thing is that colors are suitable to the individual's needs. See *Chapters 19* and *20* on *Color.*

I suggest you keep files for reference.

4. CUSTOMER AWARENESS

Become keenly aware of customer needs and types, both practical and emotional. It is also very essential that you are able to get along with people and make friends, and inspire customers with your know-all, efficiency and reliability.

5. HABITS

You must maintain a satisfactory level of performance at all times, and have a systematic, scientific method that others may follow. In other words, if a sales person or instructor is employed, you train, teach and encourage her in your method of proficiency. The sale of merchandise is really your end result, and the reputation of your business depends upon how well your customers are satisfied with their finished product.

6. ADVERTISING

I suggest you try leaflets from door to door, or a newspaper advertisement with a special attraction for opening. It need not be too elaborate—perhaps a small give-away token, a tape measure with the shop's address. With knitting taking the lead in women's hobbies, the news of the opening will soon circulate.

For your displays, ask for photo releases, mat and copy services from your manufacturers. Try to obtain models, or make one or two with quick selling-appeal. Particularly study costs of materials to ascertain greater percentage of gain. AND, to my mind, there are no better forms of advertising than word-of-mouth from a satisfied customer and your own appearance, when you are trying to sell your merchandise. Your correct styling, color and material will help establish a good customer-relationship. What if you are on the heavy side? So may be your customer. It's a fallacy to think that knits should only be worn by the very slim. How often has one heard it said that knitted skirts "cup"; so do sewn skirts and also creep up at the knees, if there isn't enough room allowed for spread.

7. BUSINESS ACUMEN

a.　You must have the ability to shoulder responsibilities.

b.　You must be able to stand behind your merchandise and your instructions.

c.　You should know how to buy the right merchandise at the right time.

d.　You should be able to perform many kinds of tasks until established, and work long hours.

e.　You should be able to keep adequate records, write a business letter, and figure discounts and interests.

Maintaining adequate records is extremely important and may provide the key to your success or failure.

TYPES OF RECORDS

a.　Keep daily record sheets from the cash register.

b.　Record cash and credit sales, layaways, purchases for both customers and self, wages, rent, utilities, incidentals, etc.

YOUR CHANCES FOR SUCCESS

I think it will be realized that not everyone has the qualifications to operate a business successfully, but today there is ample opportunity for anyone who has.

Having read the previous paragraphs, you should take stock of your personal assets and rate yourself on your qualifications. Throughout my many years as teacher and author, I have always considered, "Nothing is impossible if one makes up one's mind to succeed." True, about one third of small businesses fail the first year and approximately a sixth in the second; but if you honestly feel you can and will succeed, here are a few suggestions.

HOW TO BEGIN

Note: I have had many students who first started in a small way in their own homes, made a success of it, then branched out into a shop.

1. Find a shop in a suitable location with not a too-high rental and, if possible, near a shopping center that brings foot traffic near your doors. Ask your local Chamber of Commerce for suggestions.

2. Outfitting and Furnishing

Proper lighting is most important for helping customers and displaying merchandise.

Your basic equipment should include a sales counter, show cases, tables, comfortable chairs and a cash register; also all the necessary equipment for finishing and blocking garments.

3. Stock

Manufacturers' representatives will help you in this important aspect. Don't overload with too many brands or types of yarns. It is much better to have a sufficient supply of one type so a customer isn't kept waiting. Be careful not to overstock with slow moving numbers which are apt to tie up too much capital. And, the amount of stock to be carried depends too upon the shopkeeper's proximity to her source of supply.

4. Sources for Information

The U.S. Government Department of Commerce has informative booklets for helping small businesses. Write to Supt. of Documents, U.S. Government Printing Office, Washington, D.C.

Trade publications such as *Notion and Novelty Review, Gift and Art Buyer, Merchants Trade Journal* and the Art Needlework and Craft publications.

VOCATIONS AND OPPORTUNITIES IN THE KNITTING FIELD

One of the greatest needs of our country today is the finding of some form of industry which is not governed by automation. Hand-knitting is one of these, and there's a great need for experts along this line, as knitting, because of its relaxing qualities, is fast becoming the leading hobby of women in America.

The following are a few vocations:

Teaching in Adult Education Classes, Recreation Departments, the Y.W.C.A., and Rehabilitation Centers.

Instructresses in shops.

Designing.

Repairing and restyling hand and machine-knit garments.

Writing newspaper and magazine articles, also directions for knitting manuals.

Chapter 18, in my COMPLETE BOOK OF PROGRESSIVE KNITTING gives more information on vocations that are available.

But I cannot stress too much that in any of these positions one should have a thorough knowledge as stated in KNIT TO FIT.

CHAPTER 49

PRICES FOR ALTERATIONS, FINISHING
AND BLOCKING

I WANT TO add prices for alterations, finishing and blocking. Of course, these prices vary with the store, the clientele, the section of the country and prevailing salaries.

Sweaters

The flat rate for completely finishing sweaters is $4.00 to $5.00.

Finishing the neck with either ribbing or collar—$1.00 to $1.25.

Seams $1.50 to $2.00.

Ribbon down the front and finishing buttonholes $1.50 to $2.00.

Finishing buttonholes without ribbon 15 to 25 cents each.

Hand crocheted buttons 25 to 35 cents each.

Blocking $1.00 to $1.50.

Finishers should receive 50 to 80% of the price. The work of the finisher is extremely important, takes considerable time, and deserves adequate compensation.

Note: If the sweater has been charted correctly and knitted according to instructions, it will only be necessary to steam and flatten the seams. I feel that if sweaters did not cost so much for finishing and upkeep, women would be more enthusiastic about making other garments.

Finishing and Blocking Dresses

a.	Woolen Dresses	$12.50 to $15.00
b.	Yarn and Ribbon	$25.00 to $30.00
c.	Ribbon	$35.00 to $40.00

There is a great deal of work in putting together hand-knits.

Blocking and Cleaning Dresses

    a. Yarn $3.50 to $5.00
    b. Ribbon $5.00 to $7.50

Suits may be a little more, depending upon the style.

Note: Washing knits is preferable to dry cleaning. Many call this "wet blocking." It simply means that the garment is pinned on the board immediately after washing.

Finishing, Lining and Blocking Shortie Coats

    a. Finishing $8.00 to $10.00
    b. Lining $8.00 to $10.00
    c. Blocking $2.50 to $3.50

Alterations for Machine Knits

    a. Shortening the bottom of a skirt $ 3.50 to $ 5.00
    b. Making a 2-piece from a 1-piece $12.50 to $15.00
    c. Lengthening skirts $10.00 to $12.50

Prices of Hand-knits

(These are prices in exclusive stores.)
    a. Wool and novelty yarns $175.00 and up.
    b. Ribbon $225 and up.

    (and as much as $400.00 and more for some very special orders)

Prices for Knitters

If you employ knitters, there is quite a difference in prices— for average-weight yarn, $1.25 to $1.50 a ball is a fair price. In some localities, knitters are paid by the yard, ¾ to 1 cent. For ribbon knits, $65.00 and up, depending upon the style of the garment. Of course, all the finishing has to be done afterwards.

How to Mark-up for Trade

Figure your cost—that is the material and the labor—then mark-up 50%. That is the wholesale price. The 50% allows for your overhead. Then if you sell to the trade, their mark-up is 50% more than they paid to you. And don't forget the 2% discount allowed for 10 days, etc., and make sure what each buyer means by "10 days." I have known the time to be manipulated to about two months.

CHAPTER 50

CHANGING COLORS

HAND-KNITTING—KNITTING AND WEAVING AT THE SAME TIME

WHETHER ONE considers patterns of two or more colors of Scottish origin, Fair Isle, so named, or one of the Swedish Homesloyds, it doesn't make much difference. However, it should be stated that each province of Sweden has its own particular pattern, and if a person from the North visits the South, it is possible to tell from which province she came, by merely looking at her mittens.

Many knitters have difficulty with this type of knitting, changing and attaching the different colored threads, as well as having long, unsightly loops at the back of the work. This isn't necessary, if one learns to *knit* and *weave* at the same time.

Before starting any two-colored design, learn how to carry and fasten the strands. There should never be long loose loops at the back of the work. It is possible for the colors to be woven in. Naturally, this takes a little practice, especially on the back or purl side, if not making mittens or hats, where one uses a set of needles and works on the right side. But much time will be saved as well as a neater job done, if one spends the necessary time to accomplish this.

The easiest way to change colors so that there aren't any long loops, is to use both left and right index fingers to form the stitches. In other words, knit both the American or British way, by wrapping one yarn of one color to form a stitch with the right hand, and the Continental way wrapping the other color yarn over the index finger of the left hand.

216

Method

Knit or Right Side
Carrying Threads

One strand of yarn, white, A, is held over the index finger of the left hand, the other, black, B, over the index finger of the right. To form a stitch and carry the thread, place the right-hand needle in the left-hand loop as if to knit, also taking in the white yarn, A, on the left-hand index finger, as in illustration 39.

ILLUSTRATION 39.

Complete the knit stitch.

Note: For the next stitch, don't fasten in the white strand, A, but only every 3rd or 4th stitch. It has a tendency to separate the stitches, if done every other stitch. See illustration 40.

CHANGING COLORS

If only two or three stitches have to be made, it isn't necessary to catch in the other color, but knit the stitches the conti-

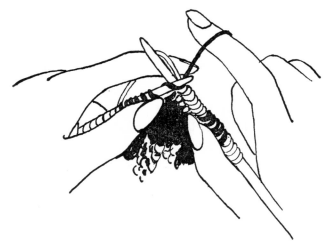

ILLUSTRATION 40.

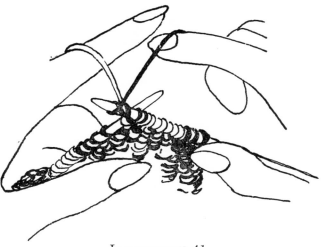

ILLUSTRATION 41.

nental way, forming the stitch with the yarn over the left index finger. However, in knitting many stitches, change the black, **B**, to the left hand, and white, **A**, to the right.

Purl on the wrong side.

The principle is the same as the knit stitch, except you are working on the front side of the work.

Put the needle in as if to purl, catching or fastening in the strand, white, **A**, on the left-hand index finger. (See illustration 41.) Complete the purl stitch.

Do not fasten the thread for the next stitch, but every 3rd or 4th stitch, as for knitting. See illustration 42.

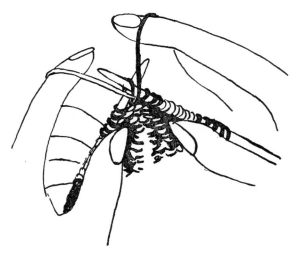

ILLUSTRATION 42.

Note: Work the pattern according to the chart. One square corresponds to a stitch. To know the necessary number of stitches, the number must be divisible by the number for each pattern. See illustration 43. (Twenty-five stitches for one.)

Fair Isle or Scandinavian on Machine

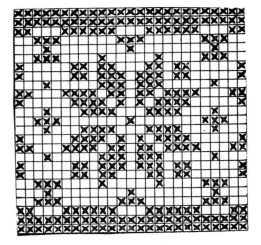

ILLUSTRATION 43.

ILLUSTRATION 44.

Method

   a. Place the needles in rest position for color, B.

   b. Place color, A, yarn over all needles, and knit one row.

   c. Place all needles in resting position.

   d. Return the slide to the beginning of the row.

   e. Leave the needles with color, A, stitches in rest position.

   f. Place the needles in previous rest position, in working position.

   g. Place color, B, yarn over all the needles.

   h. Knit one row.

   i. Continue the next rows, in the same manner, following the chart for your pattern.

GOOD LUCK!

ANSWERS

Chapter 2

WHAT TO LOOK FOR IN YOUR FUNDAMENTALS

1. You should have no difficulty with the garter stitch and do not cast on stitches with a larger needle. This makes the bottom loops too loose.
2. Does there seem to be a difference in the look of rows in your stockinette stitch? It is more than possible that you are purling looser than you knit. Tighten tension.
3. Many women knit ribbing loosely. Be especially cognizant of this fact and watch your tension. Does the 2nd stitch of your K. 2, P. 2 look larger? Increase the tension when changing stitches.
4. Always decrease at the very edge, not one stitch in, and watch out not to have apparent holes in your increasing. You may have placed your needle in between the stitches, not directly in a stitch.
5. Did you bind off loosely? Is the edge elastic?

   When binding off for shaping which is hidden in a seam, it is permissible to bind off with knit stitches; but, for ribbing, moss stitch, etc., always bind off as you would if you were working the next row. Did you bind off your ribbing correctly?

Chapter 6

MAN'S MEASUREMENTS—BACK

½ Waist—19 inches
½ Chest—21 inches
Waist-to-Underarm—11 inches

½ Armscye—10½ inches
Shoulder-to-Shoulder—17 inches
Stitch gauge—6 stitches to the inch

Method

1. 19 ins. × 6 sts. to the inch = 114 sts. for the ribbing.
2. 21 ins. × 6 sts. to the inch = 126 sts. for the body.
3. 126 sts. minus 114 sts. leaves 12 sts.
4. 12 into 114 sts. is 9½; therefore, increase first in the 9th st. then in the 10th st. on the first row after the ribbing.

SLIPOVER

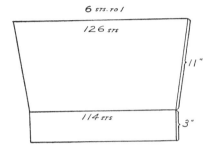

6 *sts. to 1*

126 *sts*

11"

114 *sts*

3"

DIAGRAM 83.

CARDIGAN

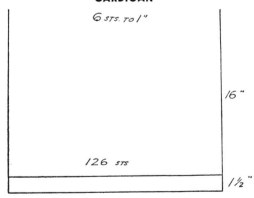

6 *sts. to 1"*

16"

126 *sts*

1½"

DIAGRAM 84.

WOMAN'S MEASUREMENTS—BACK

½ Waist—14 inches
½ Bust—18 inches
Waist-to-Underarm—8 inches
½ Armscye—9½ inches
Shoulder-to-Shoulder—14½ inches
Stitch Gauge—7 stitches to the inch

Method

1. 14 ins. × 7 sts. to the inch = 98 sts. for the ribbing.
2. 18 ins. × 7 sts. to the inch = 126 sts. for the body.
3. 126 sts. minus 98 sts. leaves 28 sts.
4. 28 into 98 sts. is 3½; therefore, increase first in the 3rd st. then in the 4th st. on the first row after the ribbing.

SLIPOVER

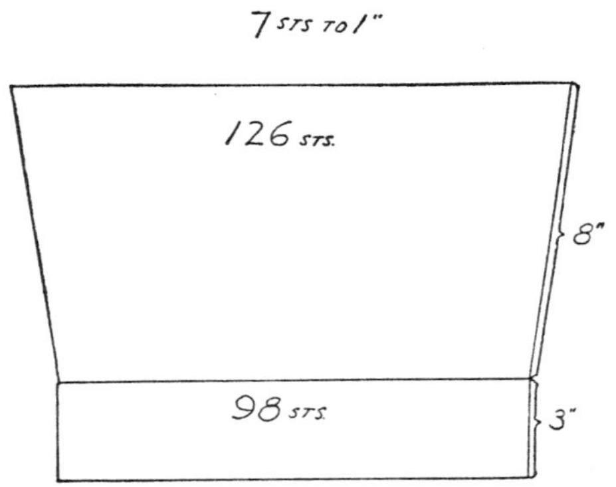

7 *sts to 1"*

126 *sts.*

8"

98 *sts*

3"

DIAGRAM 85.

CARDIGAN

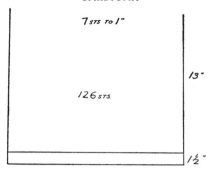

DIAGRAM 86.

CHAPTER 7

SHAPING OF ARMHOLES OR ARMSCYES

MAN

1. Shoulder-to-shoulder measurement is 17 ins. × 6 sts. to the inch = 102 sts.
2. ½ chest measurement is 126 sts. minus shoulder sts., 102, leaves 24 sts. to take off at both armholes (12 at each).
3. Bind off 6 sts. at the beginning of the next 2 rows, then knit 2 together at the beginning and end of the next 6 knitted rows.
4. Knit even to ½ the armhole measurement, 10½ ins., measuring around.

SLIPOVER

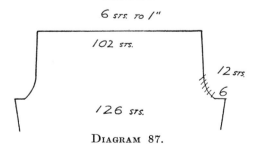

DIAGRAM 87.

CARDIGAN

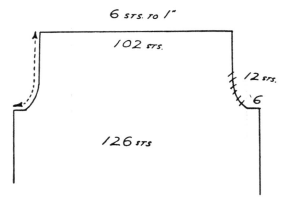

DIAGRAM 88.

WOMAN

1. Shoulder-to-shoulder measurement is $14\frac{1}{2}$ ins. $\times$ 7 sts. to the inch $=$ 102 sts.
2. $\frac{1}{2}$ bust measurement, 126 sts. minus shoulder sts., 102, is 24 sts. to take off at both armholes, 12 at each.
3. Bind off 6 sts. at the beginning of the next 2 rows, then knit 2 together at the beginning and end of the next 6 knitted (front) rows.
4. Knit even to $\frac{1}{2}$ the armhole measurement, $9\frac{1}{2}$ inches, measuring around.

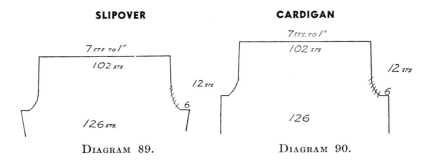

SLIPOVER   CARDIGAN

DIAGRAM 89.   DIAGRAM 90.

CHAPTER 9

SHAPING SHOULDERS

MAN

Sts. for Shoulder—102 sts.
Stitch Gauge—6 sts. to the inch, 4 slopes.

1. SLIPOVER SWEATER WITH OPENING

Shoulders for round, oval, square or "V" necklines.
 Diagrams are self-explanatory.

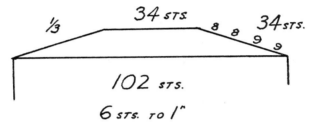

DIAGRAM 91.

2. SLIPOVER SWEATER WITHOUT AN OPENING

Shoulders for high round and turtle-necklines.

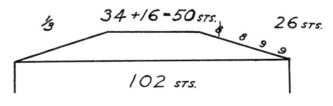

DIAGRAM 92.

3. CARDIGAN OF GENERAL STYLING

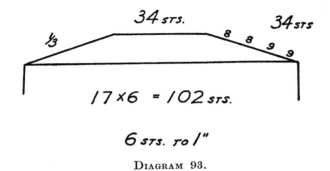

$$17 \times 6 = 102 \text{ sts.}$$

6 STS. TO 1"

DIAGRAM 93.

WOMAN

Sts. for Shoulder—102 sts.
Stitch Gauge—7 sts. to the inch, 5 slopes.

1. SLIPOVER SWEATER WITH OPENING

Shoulders for round, square, oval or "V" necklines.

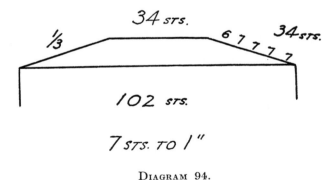

102 STS.

7 STS. TO 1"

DIAGRAM 94.

2. SLIPOVER SWEATER WITHOUT AN OPENING

Shoulders for high, round and turtle-necklines.

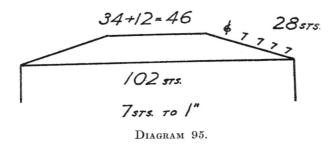

DIAGRAM 95.

3. CARDIGAN OF GENERAL STYLING

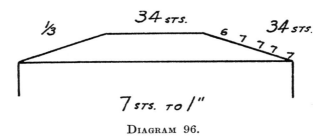

DIAGRAM 96.

CHAPTER 12

FRONTS OF CARDIGANS PLACING THE POSITION OF POCKETS

MAN

Method

1. Total back—126 sts.
2. ½ of 126 sts. is 63, even number, 64 sts.
3. ½ width of band is 4 sts. plus 64 sts. is 68 sts.

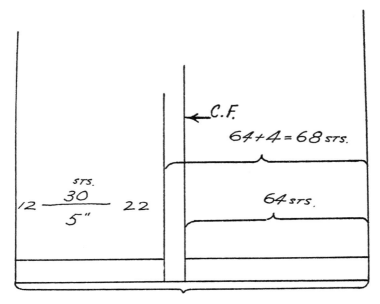

DIAGRAM 97.

POCKET

Method

1. 5 inches = 30 sts., at 6 sts. to the inch.
2. 64 minus 30 sts. leaves 34 sts.
3. $\frac{2}{3}$ of 34 sts. is 22 sts. to the center front.
4. $\frac{1}{3}$ is 12 sts. to the side seam.

WOMAN

Method

1. Total back—126 sts.
2. $\frac{1}{2}$ of 126 sts. is 63, even number, 64 sts.
3. $\frac{1}{2}$ width of band is 4 sts. plus 64 sts. = 68 sts.

POCKET

Method

1. 4 ins. = 28 sts., at 7 sts. to the inch.
2. ⅔ of 36 sts. is 24 sts. to the center front.
3. ⅓ is 12 sts. to the side seam.

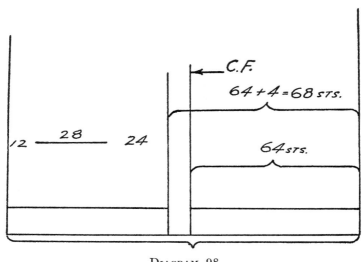

DIAGRAM 98.

CHAPTER 13

HIGH ROUND NECKLINES

MAN

1. HIGH ROUND NECKLINE WITH OPENING (SLIPOVER)

Method

(a) 102 sts. for shoulders. Knit ½ way, 51 sts. 51 sts. minus 34 sts. for the shoulder leaves 17 sts.

(b) Bind off 9 sts. the first row, then knit 2 together, every front row, 8 times.

If armhole isn't the same as the back, knit even until the same length.

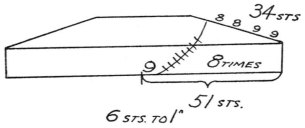

Diagram 99.

2. HIGH ROUND NECK WITHOUT OPENING (SLIPOVER)

Don't work the last slope of the shoulder at the back.

Method

   (a) 102 sts. for the shoulders. Knit ½ way, 51 sts. minus 26 sts. for shoulder = 25 sts.
   (b) Bind off 13 sts. the first row, then knit 2 together, every front row, 12 times.

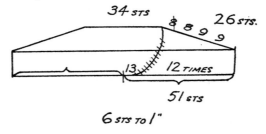

Diagram 100.

3. HIGH ROUND NECK FOR CARDIGAN

Method

   (a) 56 sts. minus ½ the width of the band, 4 sts. = 52 sts. to the center front.
   (b) 52 sts. minus shoulder sts., 34, leaves 18 sts. Bind off 9 sts. and 2 together, 9 times, but :—

(c) Add ½ the width of the band, 4 sts., to the first bind off, 9 plus 4 = 13 sts.

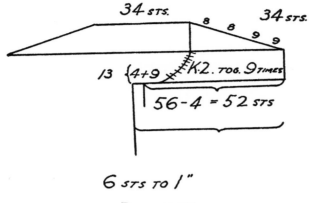

34 STS.   8   8   34 STS.
                        9 9
13 {4+9 K.2. TOG. 9 TIMES
    56 − 4 = 52 STS

6 STS TO 1"

DIAGRAM 101.

WOMAN
1. HIGH ROUND NECK WITH OPENING (SLIPOVER)

Method

(a) 102 sts. for shoulder. Knit ½ way, 51 sts. 51 minus 34 sts. for shoulder = 17 sts.

(b) Bind off 9 sts. the first row, then knit 2 together, every front row, 8 times.

If the armhole isn't the same length as the back, knit even until the same length.

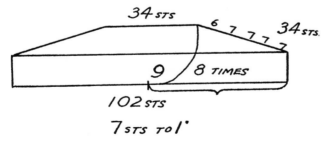

34 STS   6 7 7 7   34 STS.
         9 / 8 TIMES
102 STS
7 STS TO 1"

DIAGRAM 102.

2. HIGH ROUND NECK WITHOUT OPENING (SLIPOVER)

Do not work the last slope of the shoulder at the back.

Method

(a) 102 sts. for shoulders. Knit ½ way, 51 sts. 51 sts. minus 28 sts. for the shoulder leaves 23 sts.

(b) Bind off 12 sts. the first row, then knit 2 together, every front row, 11 times.

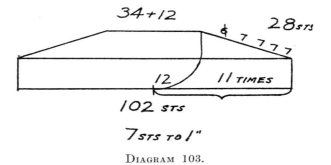

DIAGRAM 103.

3. HIGH ROUND NECK FOR CARDIGAN

Method

(a) 56 sts. minus ½ the width of the band, 4 sts., is 52 sts. to the center front.

(b) 52 sts. minus shoulder sts., 34, leaves 18 sts. Bind off 9 sts. and knit 2 together, 9 times, but :—

(c) Add ½ the width of the band, 4 sts., to the first bind off, 9 plus 4 = 13 sts.

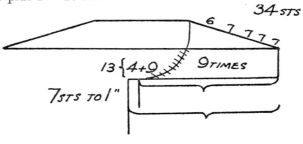

DIAGRAM 104.

CHAPTER 14

"V" NECKLINES

WOMAN

The diagrams are self-explanatory.

1.   2 inches after the first bind off at the armhole, or when all the armhole sts. have been decreased, knit 2 together, every front row.

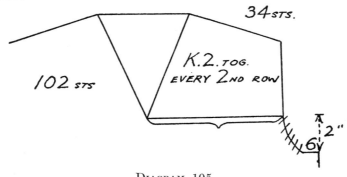

DIAGRAM 105.

2.   At the first bind off at the armhole, knit 2 together, every 4th row, i.e., every 2nd front row.

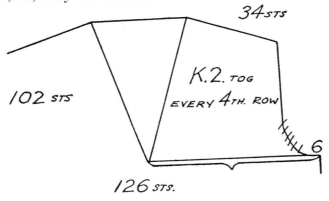

DIAGRAM 106.

3. Just above the waist line, knit 2 together, every 8th row, i.e., every 4th front row.

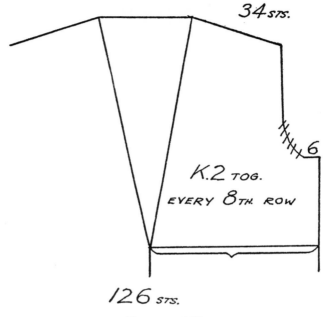

DIAGRAM 107.

CHAPTER 15

LONG SLEEVES

MAN

Measurements

Wrist—8 inches
Upperarm—13 inches
Sleeve length—20 inches
Stitch Gauge—6 sts. to the inch

Method

1. Wrist—8 ins. plus 1 inch = 9 ins. 9 ins. × 6 = 54 sts. Add 2 sts. for K. 2, P. 2, making 56 sts.
2. 2 ins. added to the first row after the ribbing is 56 sts. plus 12 sts., which = 68 sts.
3. Upperarm is 13 ins. plus 3 ins. = 16 ins. × 6 sts. to the inch = 96 sts.
4. 96 sts. minus 68 sts. leaves 28 sts. to be increased—14 sts. at each side.
5. Increase 1 st. at the beginning and end of row, every inch, 14 times.

CAP

(a) Bind off 6 sts. at the beginning of next 2 rows, then knit 2 together at the beginning and end of each front row, until 4½ inches of sts.—28 sts.—remain, then bind off 2 sts., until 2 inches, 12 sts., are left.
(b) Bind off.

WOMAN

Measurements

Wrist—6 inches
Upperarm—11 inches
Sleeve length—17½ inches
Stitch Gauge—7 sts. to the inch

Method

1. Wrist—6 ins. plus 1 inch = 7 ins. 7 × 7 sts. to the inch = 49 sts., even number, 50 sts.
2. 1 in. added to the first row after the ribbing, 58 sts.
3. Upperarm is 11 ins. plus 2 ins. = 13 ins. × 7 sts. to the inch = 91 sts., even number—92 sts.
4. 92 sts. minus 58 sts. = 34 sts., 17 sts. at each side.
5. Increase 1 st. at the beginning and end of row, every ¾ inch, 17 times.
6. Knit even until underarm measurement is reached.

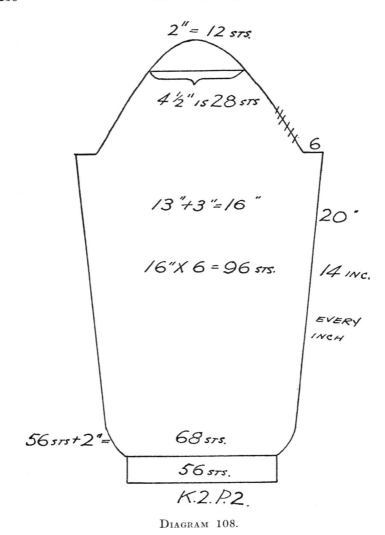

DIAGRAM 108.

CAP

(a) Bind off at 6 sts. at the beginning of the next 2 rows, then knit 2 together at the beginning and end of each front row, until $3\frac{1}{2}$ inches of sts., 26 sts., remain, then bind off 2 sts. until 2 ins., 14 sts., are left.

(b) Bind off.

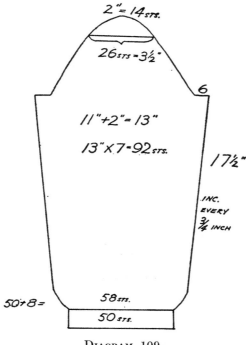

$2'' = 14$ STS.

26 STS $= 3\frac{1}{2}''$

6

$11'' + 2'' = 13''$

$13'' \times 7 = 92$ STS.

$17\frac{1}{2}''$

INC. EVERY $\frac{3}{4}$ INCH

$50 + 8 =$

58 STS.

50 STS.

DIAGRAM 109.

CHAPTER 16

SHORT SLEEVE

Diagram is self-explanatory.

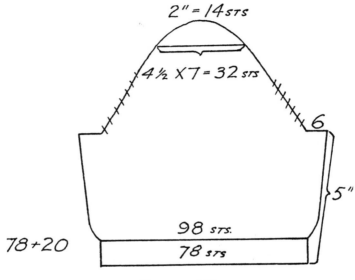

DIAGRAM 110.

CHAPTER 21

SLEEVELESS SWEATERS

MAN

SWEATER WITH SET-IN SLEEVES

Measurements

½ Waist—19 inches
½ Chest—21 inches
Shoulder-to-Shoulder—17 inches
½ Armhole—10½ inches
Stitch Gauge—6 sts. to the inch

Diagram is self-explanatory.

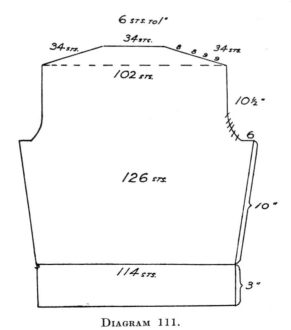

DIAGRAM 111.

SLEEVELESS SWEATER

Diagram shows necessary changes.

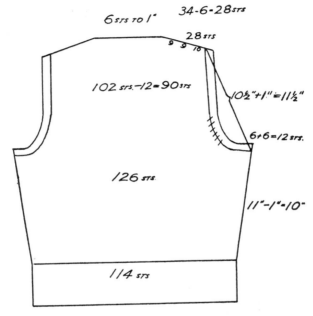

6 sts to 1"   34-6-28 sts

28 sts

9 9 10

102 sts.-12=90 sts

10½"+1."=11½"

6+6=12 sts.

126 sts.

11"-1"=10"

114 sts

DIAGRAM 112.

WOMAN

SWEATER WITH SET-IN SLEEVES

Measurements

½ Waist—14 inches
½ Bust—18 inches
Waist-to-Underarm—8 inches
Shoulder-to-Shoulder—14½ inches
½ Armhole—9½ inches
Stitch Gauge—7 sts. to the inch

Diagram is self-explanatory.

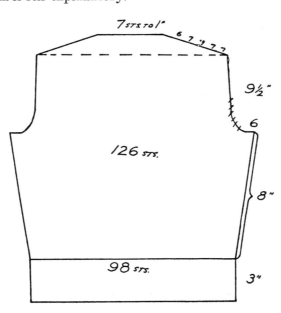

7 sts to 1"

6 7 9 7 7

9½"

6

126 sts.

8"

98 sts.

3"

DIAGRAM 113.

SLEEVELESS SWEATER

Diagram shows necessary changes.

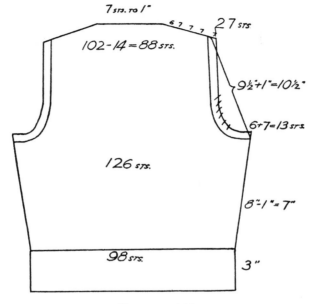

7 sts. to 1"

2 7 sts

6 7 7 7

102 - 14 = 88 sts.

9½ + 1" = 10½"

6 + 7 = 13 sts

126 sts.

8" ÷ 1" = 7"

98 sts.

3 "

DIAGRAM 114.

SLEEVELESS SWEATER WITH 5 CABLES

Cables to be evenly spaced, using P. 2, K. 6, P. 2.

Measurements

½ Waist—19 inches
Underarm-to-Waist—11 inches
½ Chest—21 inches
Stitch Gauge—6 sts. to the inch

Method

1. 126 sts. plus 10 sts. for 5 cables = 136 sts.
2. 5 cables using 10 sts. each = 50 sts.
3. 136 sts. minus 50 sts. = 86 sts. for 6 spaces; therefore K. 14 for 4 spaces, and K. 15 for each end.

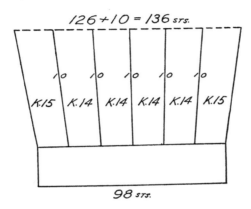

DIAGRAM 115.

CHAPTER 22

WOMAN'S WESKIT WITH SQUARE NECKLINE

Measurements

½ Waist—14 inches
½ Bust—18 inches
Waist-to-Underarm—8 inches
Shoulder-to-Shoulder—14 inches
½ Armhole—9½ inches
Stitch Gauge—7 sts. to the inch

If you have understood the other lessons, the diagrams are self-explanatory.

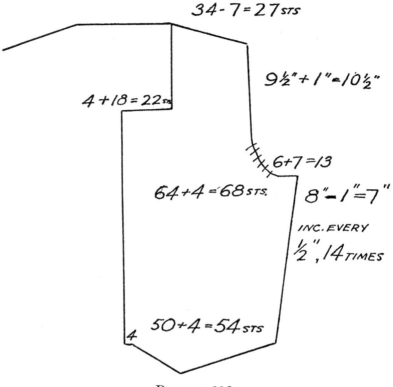

$34-7=27$ sts

$9\frac{1}{2}"+1"=10\frac{1}{2}"$

$4+18=22$ sts

$6+7=13$

$64+4=68$ sts.

$8"-1"=7"$

INC. EVERY
$\frac{1}{2}"$, 14 TIMES

$50+4=54$ sts

4

DIAGRAM 116.

$50+4=54$ sts.

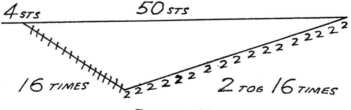

4 STS

50 STS

16 TIMES

2 TOG 16 TIMES

DIAGRAM 117.

CHAPTER 23

WOMAN'S FITTED SWEATER WITH OVAL NECKLINE

Measurements

½ Waist—14 inches
½ Bust—18 inches
Waist-to-Underarm—8 inches
½ Armhole—9½ inches
Hip, 6 inches below Waist—36 inches
Stitch Gauge—7 sts. to the inch

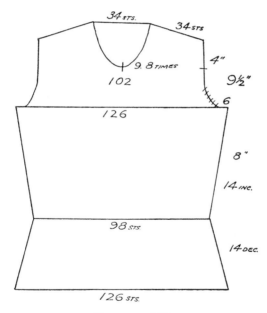

DIAGRAM 118.

Method

1. 126 sts. minus 98 sts. leaves 28 sts. 14 sts. to decrease at each side, in 6 ins.—a little less than every ½ inch.
2. Similarly, 14 sts. to be increased on each side, every ½ inch, 2 ins. even to the underarm.
3. Neckline—Oval neckline starts 4 ins. below the tip of the shoulder.

    (a) 9½ ins. minus 4 ins. leaves 5½ ins.; therefore, at 5½ inches, decrease for oval neckline, which is the same as a low, round-neckline.

    (b) 34 sts. from 51 sts. leaves 17 sts. Bind off 9 sts. and knit 2 together, 8 times.

CHAPTER 25

NECKLINES FOR EVENING SWEATERS AND BLOUSES

1. WIDE, OFF-SHOULDER, SCOOP NECKLINE

Measurements

Shoulder-to-Shoulder—15 ins.
Neckline—6 ins. deep at the center and ends, 2 inches below the tip of the shoulder
Stitch Gauge— 7 sts. to the inch
                    10 rows to the inch

Method

1. 15 ins. × 7 sts. to the inch = 105 sts., use 104 sts. ½ of 104 is 52 sts. to the center.
2. 6 ins. minus 2 inches to the tip of the shoulder leaves 4 ins. in which to decrease 52 sts.
3. 10 rows to the inch × 4 = 40 rows, or 20 rows on which to bind off.
4. 20 into 52 goes twice and 12 sts. over; therefore, bind off 3 sts. at the neck edge, 12 times, and 2 sts., 8 times.

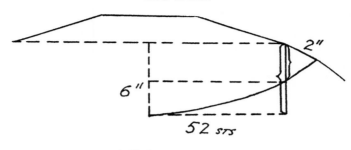

DIAGRAM 119.

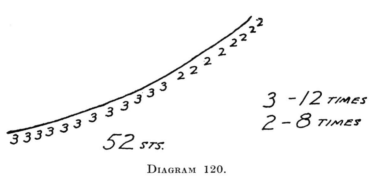

3 - 12 TIMES
2 - 8 TIMES

DIAGRAM 120.

CHAPTER 26

2. WIDE, ON-SHOULDER OVAL NECKLINE

Measurements: the same as Chapter 25.

The neckline starts 5 inches below the tip of the shoulder, and uses 2 shoulder slopes.

Method

1. 15 ins. $\times$ 7 sts. to the inch = 105 sts., use 104 sts. ½ of 104 is 52 sts. to the center, 7 sts. to the inch, therefore 5 shoulder slopes.

2. Depth of neckline 5 ins. $\times$ 10 rows to the inch $=$ 50 rows, or 25 rows on which to decrease at the front edge.

3. 52 sts. minus 14 shoulder sts. leaves 38 sts. to be decreased in 25 rows. Use 1 row for the first bind off, therefore, 38 minus 24 $=$ 14 sts. to be bound off at the beginning, then knit 2 together, at the front edge, every other row, 24 times.

4. Bind off the 2 shoulder slopes.

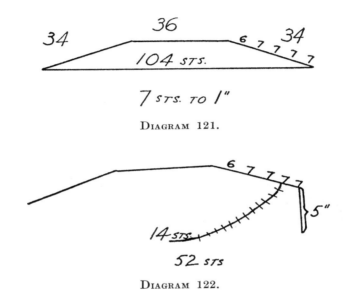

DIAGRAM 121.

DIAGRAM 122.

3. WIDE, SQUARE ON-SHOULDER NECKLINE

Neckline starts 6 ins. below the tip of the shoulder and uses 3 shoulder slopes.

Method

1. 3 shoulder slopes $=$ 21 sts., therefore 42 sts. for both.
2. 104 sts. minus 42 sts. leaves 62 sts. for the neckline.
3. Knit 21 sts. Bind off 62 sts.
4. Knit even on remaining 21 sts. until the shoulder is reached.

5. Shape the shoulder.
6. Knit the other side, reversing the shaping.

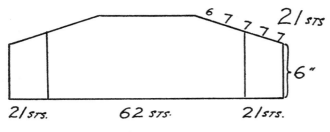

DIAGRAM 123.

CHAPTER 27

CAP SLEEVES

1. CAP STRAIGHT OUT FROM THE SHOULDER

Measurements

Shoulder-to-Shoulder—15 inches
½ Bust Measurement—18 inches
Cap—3 inches
Stitch gauge—7 sts. to the inch, 10 rows to the inch.

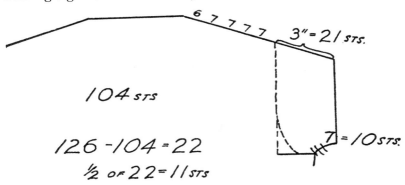

DIAGRAM 124.

Method

1. 18 ins. × 7 sts. to the inch = 126 sts.
2. 15 ins. × 7 sts. to the inch = 104 sts. for the shoulders.
3. 126 sts. minus 104 sts. is 22 sts. to take off for armscyes, 11 sts. for each.
4. 3-inch cap is 21 sts.
5. 21 sts. minus 11 sts. leaves 10 sts. to add at the underarm, 1 st., every other row, 3 times, then 7 sts. all at one time.

2. CAP SLIGHTLY FITTING AT THE UPPERARM

Method

1. Bind off 2 sts., every other row, 9 times, and 3 sts. once, making 20 rows.
2. 20 rows at 10 rows to an inch = 2 ins.
3. This is 2 ins. less than ½ required width of straight cap, or ½ the armhole measurement.

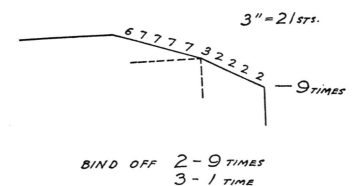

DIAGRAM 125.

CHAPTER 29

SKIRTS

STRAIGHT SKIRTS

Measurements

Waist—29 inches

Hips—39 inches (9 inches below the waist)

Length—31 inches, minus 1 inch for crochet leaves 30 inches knitted length

Stitch Gauge—6 sts. to the inch

Method

1. Waist is 29 ins. $\times$ 6 sts. to the inch = 174 sts., nearest 10, 170 sts.
2. 39 ins. plus 4 ins. = 43 ins. $\times$ 6 sts. to the inch = 258 sts., nearest 10, 260 sts.
3. Width at the bottom is 43 ins. plus 10 ins. = 53 ins. $\times$ 6 sts. to the inch = 318 sts., nearest 10, 320 sts.
4. Decreases

    (a) Bottom to hips—320 sts. minus 260 sts. leaves 60 sts. or 6 decreases of 10 sts. each.

    (b) 21 ins. to the hips—6 into 21 ins. goes 3 and 3 ins. over; therefore, there are 3 decreases of 4 ins. and 3 decreases of 3 ins.

    (c) Hips to waist—260 sts. minus 170 sts. leaves 90 sts. or 9 decreases of 10 sts. each.

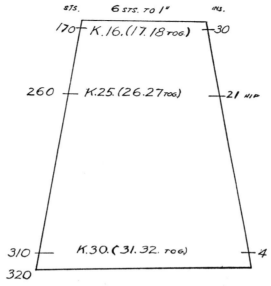

DIAGRAM 126.

6 sts to the inch

Sts		Ins	
170		30	
170	K.16 (17.18 tog.)	29½	last ½ inch even
180	K.17 (18.19 tog.)	29	
190	K.18 (19.20 tog.)	28	
200	K.19 (20.21 tog.)	27	
210	K.20 (21.22 tog.)	26	
220	K.21 (22.23 tog.)	25	
230	K.22 (23.24 .tog.)	24	
240	K.23 (24.25 tog.)	23	
250	K.24 (25.26 tog.)	22	
260	K.25 (26.27 tog.)	21	Hip
270	K.26 (27.28 tog.)	18	
280	K.27 (28.29 tog.)	15	
290	K.28 (29.30 tog.)	12	
300	K.29 (30.31 tog.)	8	
310	K.30 (31.32 tog.)	4	
320			

DIAGRAM 127.

CHAPTER 30

STRAIGHT SKIRTS WITH DIFFERENT STITCH GAUGES

#1.

Same measurements as Chapter 29.
Stitch Gauge—7 sts. to the inch.

Method

1. Waist—29 ins. $\times$ 7 sts. to the inch $=$ 203 sts., nearest 10, 200 sts.
2. Hips—39 ins. plus 4 ins. $=$ 43 ins. $\times$ 7 sts. to the inch or 301 sts., nearest 10, 300 sts.
3. Width at the Bottom—43 ins. plus 10 ins. $=$ 53 ins. $\times$ 7 sts. to the inch or 371 sts., nearest 10, 370 sts.
4. Decreases

    (a) Bottom-to-Hips—370 sts. minus 300 sts. leaves 70 sts. or 7 decreases of 10 sts.

    (b) Hips-to-Waist—300 sts. minus 200 sts. leaves 100 sts. or 10 decreases of 10 sts. See diagrams 128 and 129.

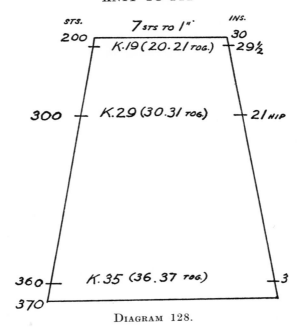

STS.   7 STS TO 1"   INS.

200   K.19 (20.21 TOG.)   30   29½

300   K.29 (30.31 TOG.)   21 HIP

360   K.35 (36.37 TOG.)   3
370

DIAGRAM 128.

7 sts to the inch

Sts		Ins	
		30	
200	K.19 (20.21 tog.)	29½	last ½ inch even
200	K.20 (21.22 tog.)	29	
210	K.21 (22.23 tog.)	28½	
220	K.22 (23.24 tog.)	28	
230	K.23 (24.25 tog.)	27	
240	K.24 (25.26 tog.)	26	
250	K.25.(26.27 tog.)	25	
260	K.26 (27.28 tog.)	24	
270	K.27 (28.29 tog.)	23	
280	K.28 (29.30 tog.)	22	
290	K.29 (30.31 tog.)	21	Hip
300	K.30 (31.32 tog.)	18	
310	K.31 (32.33 tog.)	15	
320	K.32 (33.34 tog.)	12	
330	K.33 (34.35 tog.)	9	
340	K.34 (35.36 tog.)	6	
350	K.35 (36.37 tog.)	3	
360			
370			

DIAGRAM 129.

CHAPTER 31

FLARED SKIRTS

Measurements the same as Chapter 29, allowing 1 inch for crochet in length.

Width at the Bottom—61 ins.; 20 ins. more than the necessary hip measurement of 39 plus 2 ins., or 41 ins.

Stitch Gauge—6 sts. to the inch

Method

1. Waist—29 ins. $\times$ 6 sts. to the inch = 174 sts., use 170 sts.
2. Hips—39 ins. plus 2 ins. = 41 ins. $\times$ 6 sts. to the inch = 246 sts., use 250 sts.
3. Width at the Bottom—61 ins. $\times$ 6 sts. to the inch is 366 sts., use 370 sts.
4. Decreases

   (a) Bottom to Hips—370 sts. minus 250 sts. leaves 120 sts. Cannot divide 370 evenly by 20, so decrease 10 sts. first, then 5 decreases of 20 sts., and 1 decrease of 10 sts. See diagrams 130 and 131.

   (b) Hips to Waist—250 sts. minus 170 sts. leaves 80 sts., or 8 decreases of 10 sts.

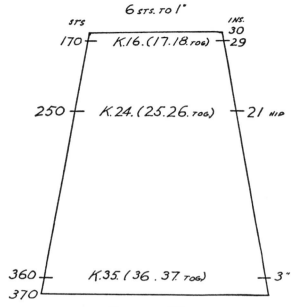

DIAGRAM 130.

6 sts to the inch

Sts		Ins	
170		30	
170	K.16 (17.18 tog.)	29	last inch even
180	K.17 (18.19 tog.(	28	
190	K.18 (19.20 tog.)	27	
200	K.19 (20.21 tog.)	26	
210	K.20 (21.22 tog.)	25	
220	K.21 (22.23 tog.)	24	
230	K.22 (23.24 tog.)	23	
240	K.23 (24.25 tog.)	22	
250	K.24 (25.26 tog.)	21	Hip
260	K.12 (13.14 tog.)	18	
280	K.13 (14.15 tog.)	15	
300	K.14 (15.16 tog.)	12	
320	K.15 (16.17 tog.)	9	
340	K.16 (17.18 tog.)	6	
360	K.35 (36.37 tog.)	3	
370			

DIAGRAM 131.

CHAPTER 32

FLARED SKIRTS WITH DIFFERENT
STITCH GAUGES

#1.

Measurements

Waist—29 ins.
Hips—39 ins. plus 4 ins. = 43 ins.
Width at the Bottom—58 ins.
Length—31 ins., 1 inch for crochet = 30 ins.
Stitch Gauge—7 sts. to the inch

Method

1. Waist—29 ins. × 7 sts. to the inch = 203 sts., use 200 sts.
2. Hips—39 ins. plus 4 ins. = 43 ins. × 7 = 301 sts., use 300 sts.
3. Width at the Bottom—43 ins. plus 15 ins. = 58 ins. × 7 = 406 sts., use 410.
4. Decreases

    (a) Bottom to Hips—410 sts. minus 300 sts. leaves 110 sts. to decrease. 5 decreases of 20 sts. and 1 decrease of 10 sts.

    (b) Hips to Waist—300 sts. minus 200 sts. = 100 sts. or 10 decreases of 10 sts. See diagrams 132 and 133.

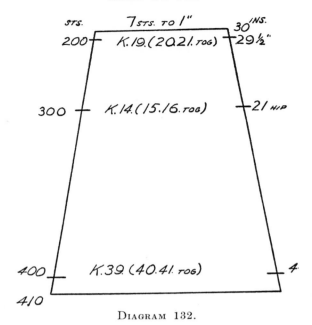

DIAGRAM 132.

7 sts to the inch

Sts		Ins	
200		30	
200	K.19 (20.21 tog.)	29½	last ½ inch even
210	K.20 (21.22 tog.)	29	
220	K.21 (22.23 tog.)	28½	
230	K.22 (23.24 tog.)	28	
240	K.23 (24.25 tog.)	27	
250	K.24 (25.26 tog.)	26	
260	K.25 (26.27 tog.)	25	
270	K.26 (27.28 tog.)	24	
280	K.27 (28.29 tog.)	23	
290	K.28 (29.30 tog.)	22	
300	K.14 (15.16 tog.)	21	Hip
320	K.15 (16.17 tog.)	18	
340	K.16 (17.18 tog.)	15	
360	K.17 (18.19 tog.)	12	
380	K.18 (19.20 tog.)	8	
400	K.39 (40.41 tog.)	4	
410			

DIAGRAM 133.

#2.

Same measurements as #1, but Stitch Gauge—8 sts. to the inch.

Method

1. Waist—29 ins. × 8 sts. to the inch = 232 sts., use 230 sts.
2. Hips—39 ins. plus 4 ins. = 43 ins. × 8 or 344 sts., use 340.
3. Width at the Bottom—53 ins. × 8 = 424, use 420 sts.
4. Decreases

    (a) Bottom to Hips—420 sts. minus 340 leaves 80 sts. or 8 decreases of 10 sts.
    (b) Hips to Waist—340 sts. minus 230 sts. leaves 110 sts., 11 decreases of 10 sts., or 5 decreases of 20 sts. and 1 decrease of 10 sts. See diagrams 134 and 135 on following page.

#3.

Measurements

Waist—29 inches
Hips—39 inches plus 2 inches = 41 inches
Width at the Bottom—61 inches
Stitch Gauge—8 sts. to the inch

Method

1. Waist—29 ins. × 8 sts. to the inch = 232 sts., use 230 sts.
2. Hips—39 ins. plus 2 ins. = 41 ins. × 8 is 328 sts., use 330 sts.
3. Bottom—41 ins. plus 20 = 61 ins. × 8 = 488 sts., use 490.
4. Decreases

    (a) Bottom to Hips—490 sts. minus 330 sts. leaves 160 sts. 7 decreases of 20 sts., and 2 decreases of 10 sts.
    (b) Hips to Waist—330 sts. minus 230 sts. leaves 100 sts. or 10 decreases of 10 sts. each. See diagrams 136 and 137.

8 sts to the inch

Sts		Ins	
230		30	
230	K.22 (23.24 tog.)	29	last inch even
240	K.11.(12.13 tog.)	28	
260	K.12.(13.14 tog.)	27	
280	K.13 (14.15 tog.)	26	
300	K.14 (15.16 tog.)	25	
320	K.15 (16.17 tog.)	23	
340	K.33 (34.35 tog.)	21	Hip
350	K.34 (35.36 tog.)	19	
360	K.35 (36.37 tog.)	17	
370	K.36 (37.38 tog.)	15	
380	K.37 (38.39 tog.)	12	
390	K.38 (39.40 tog.)	9	
400	K.39 (40.41 tog.)	6	
410	K.40 (41.42 tog.)	3	
420			

DIAGRAM 134.

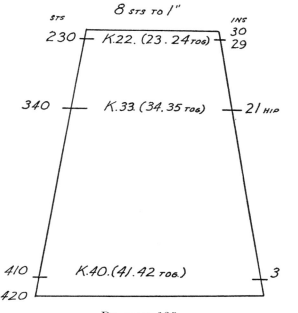

DIAGRAM 135.

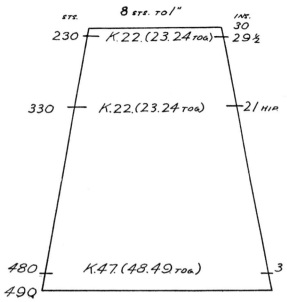

STS.   8 STS. TO 1"   INS.

230 — K.22. (23. 24 TOG) — 30 29½

330 — K.22.(23.24 TOG) — 21 HIP

480 — K.47. (48.49 TOG.) — 3
490

DIAGRAM 136.

8 sts to the inch

Sts		Ins	
230		30	
230	K.22 (23.24 tog.)	29½	last ½ inch
240		29	even
250		28½	
260	1 fewer st between	28	
270	each decrease	27	
280		26	
290		25	
300		24	
310		23	
320		22	
330	K.32 (33.34 tog.)	21	Hip
340	K.16 (17.18 tog.)	19	
360	K.17 (18.19 tog.)	17	
380	K.18 (19.20 tog.)	15	
400	K.19 (20.21 tog.)	13	
420	K.20 (21.22 tog.)	11	
440	K.21 (22.23 tog.)	9	
460	K.22 (23.24 tog.)	6	
480	K.47 (48.49 tog.)	3	
490			

DIAGRAM 137.

CHAPTER 33

GORED OR PANEL SKIRTS

12-GORED SKIRT WITH P. 2, BETWEEN

Measurements

Waist—29 inches
Hips—39 inches plus 2 inches = 41 inches
Length—31 ins. (30 inches knitted length)
Width at the Bottom—76 inches
Stitch Gauge—6 sts. to the inch

Method

1. Waist—29 ins. $\times$ 6 sts. to the inch = 174 sts.—nearest number divisible by 12 is 180 sts. 12 into 180 = 15 sts., i.e., **K. 13, P. 2.**

2. Hips—39 ins. plus 2 ins. = 41 ins. $\times$ 6 sts. to the inch makes 246 sts., divisible by 12 = 252 sts. 12 into 252 goes 21 times, i.e., **K. 19, P. 2.**

3. Width at the Bottom—76 ins. $\times$ 6 sts. to the inch = 456 sts., divisible by 12 is 38 sts., i.e., **K. 36, P. 2.**

4. Decreases in each panel or gore

   (a) Bottom to Hips—36 minus 19 leaves 17 sts. to be decreased in each panel, 2 sts. 8 times and 1 st. once. See diagrams 138 and 139.

   (b) Hips to Waist—19 sts. minus 13 sts. leaves 6 sts. to be decreased in each panel, 6 times.

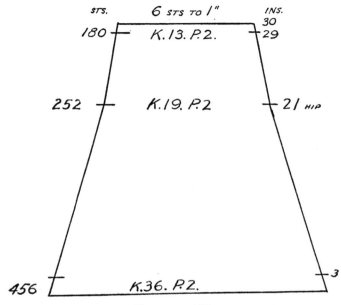

STS.   6 STS TO 1"   INS.
                          30
180 —   K.13. P.2.   — 29

252 —   K.19. P.2   — 21 HIP

456 —   K.36. P.2.   — 3

DIAGRAM 138.

6 sts to the inch

Sts		Ins	
180		30	
180	K.13.P.2.	29	last inch even
	6 decreases in each gore	28	
		27	
		26	
		24	
		22	
252	K.19.P.2.	21	
		19	
	17 sts to be decreased in	17	
	each gore.	15	
	2 sts - 8 times	13	
	1 st - once	11	
		9	
		6	
		3	
456	K.36.P.2.		

DIAGRAM 139.

CHAPTER 34

GORED SKIRTS WITH DIFFERENT STITCH GAUGES

#1.

Same measurements as Chapter 33.

8-GORED SKIRT

Width at the Bottom—80 inches
Stitch Gauge—7 sts. to the inch

Method

1. Waist—29 ins. $\times$ 7 sts. to the inch = 203 sts., nearest number divisible by 8 is 200 sts. 8 into 200 goes 25 times, i.e., K. 23, P. 2.
2. Hips—39 ins. plus 2 ins. = 41 ins. $\times$ 7 sts. to the inch = 287 sts., nearest number divisible by 8 is 288 sts. 8 into 288 goes 36 times, i.e., K. 34, P. 2.
3. Width at the Bottom—80 ins. $\times$ 7 sts. to the inch = 560 sts., divisible by 8 is 70 sts., i.e., K. 68, P. 2.
4. Decreases

   (a) Bottom to Hips—34 sts. from 68 sts. leaves 34 sts. to be decreased in each gore; 3 sts. in each gore, 10 times, and 2 sts. in each gore, 2 times. See diagrams.
   (b) Hips to Waist—23 sts. from 34 sts. leaves 11 sts. to decrease in each gore, 1 stitch in each panel 11 times, first at one side, then the other.

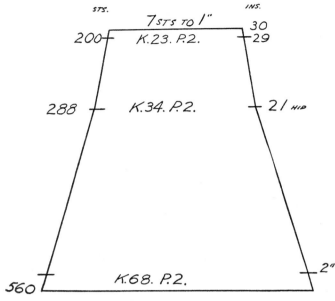

DIAGRAM 140.

7 sts to the inch

Sts		Ins	
200		30	last inch even
200	K.23.P.2.	29	
		28	
	5 decreases of 2 sts.	27	
	1 decrease of 1 st.	26	
		25	
		23	
288	K.34.P.2.	21	hip
		20	
		19	
		18	
		16	
		14	
	10 decreases of 3 sts.	12	
	2 decreases of 2 sts.	10	
		8	
		6	
		4	
		2	
560	K.68.P.2.		

DIAGRAM 141.

6-GORED SKIRT WITH P. 1, BETWEEN

Measurements

Waist—29 inches
Hips—39 inches plus 2 inches is 41 inches
Length—31 inches (30 inches knitted length)
Width at the Bottom—76 inches
Stitch Gauge—7 sts. to the inch

Method

1. Waist—29 inches $\times$ 7 sts. to the inch = 203 sts., nearest number divisible by 6 is 204 sts.; 6 into 204 goes 34 times, i.e., K. 33, P. 1.

2. Hips—39 ins. plus 2 ins. = 41 ins. $\times$ 7 sts. to the inch is 287 sts., nearest number divisible by 6 is 288 sts. 6 into 288 goes 48 times, i.e., K. 47, P. 1.

3. Width at the Bottom—76 ins. $\times$ 7 sts. to the inch = 532 sts., nearest number divisible by 6 is 534 sts., 89 times, i.e., K. 88, P. 1.

4. Decreases

    (a) Bottom to Hips—47 sts. from 88 sts. leaves 41 sts., i.e., 10 decreases of 4 sts. in each gore and 1 decrease of 1 st. First row of decreasing is as follows:—K. 1, K. 2 tog., K. 26, K. 2 tog., K. 26, K. 2 tog., K. 26, K. 2 tog., K. 1 (88 sts.), P. 1.

    (b) Hips to Waist—33 sts. from 47 sts. leaves 14 sts.; 2 sts. to decrease in each gore, 7 times.

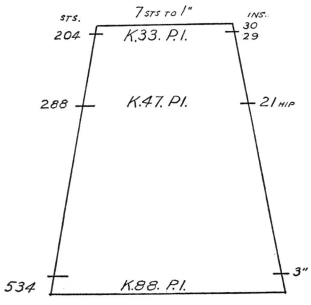

STS.   7 STS TO 1"   INS.

204 ┤   K.33. P.I.   ├ 30 / 29

288 ┤   K.47. PI.   ├ 21 HIP

534 ┤   K.88. P.I.   ├ 3"

DIAGRAM 142.

7 sts to the inch

Sts		Ins	
204		30	last inch even
204	K.33.P.1.	29	
		28	
	7 decreases of 2 sts.	27	
		26	
		25	
		24	
		23	
288	K.47.P.1.	21	hip
		20	
		19	
		18	
		16	
		14	
	10 decreases of 4 sts.	12	
	1 decrease of 1 st.	10	
		8	
		6	
		3	
534	K.88.P.1.		

DIAGRAM 143.

Chapter 35

PLEATED SKIRTS

Measurements the same as Chapter 34.

Width at the Bottom—76 inches, 2 inch pleats
Stitch Gauge—7 sts. to the inch; therefore, 14 sts. in each pleat,
    28 sts. in the knit and purl pleats together.

Method

1. Width at the Bottom—76 ins. × 7 sts. to the inch = 532 sts.
   28 into 532 goes 19 times, making 38 ribs altogether.
2. Hips—39 inches plus 4 inches = 43 inches × 7 sts. to the inch
   is 301 sts.—use 304 sts. 38 into 304 goes 8 times; therefore
   there are K. 8, P. 8 at the hips.
3. Waist—29 ins. plus 2 ins. = 31, × 7 sts. to the inch = 217
   sts. May be divisible by 19 or 38 sts.; use 228 sts. 38 into 228
   goes 6 times, i.e., K. 6, P. 6 at the waist.

Note: Suggest the higher number for pleated skirts.

4. Decreases

   (a) 12 decreases first in the knit ribs, then in the purl to the
   hips.
   (b) Alternately decrease in the knit ribs, then the purl, every
   2 ins. to the waist. See diagrams 144 and 145.

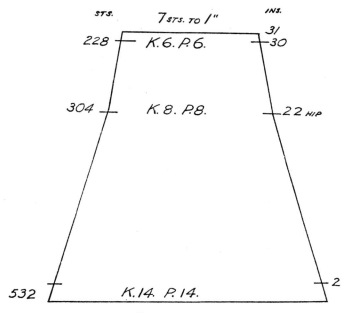

DIAGRAM 144.

<u>7 sts to the inch</u>

Sts		Ins	
228		31	
228	K.6.P.6.	30	last inch even
		28	
		26	
		24	
304	K.8.P.8.	22	Hip
		21	
		20	
		18	
		16	
		14	
		12	
		10	
		8	
		6	
	19 pleats of :-	4	
		2	
532	K.14.P.14.		

DIAGRAM 145.

CHAPTER 37

RIBBON OR MACHINE-KNIT SKIRTS

4-GORED RIBBON SKIRT OR 4-GORED MACHINE-KNIT SKIRT

Measurements

Waist—29 inches
Hips—39 inches plus 4 inches = 43 inches
Width at the Bottom—53 inches
Length—31 inches; ½-inch crochet allowance in length, 30½ inches
½-inch each side seam allowance for each panel or gore
Stitch Gauge—5 sts. to the inch

Method

1. Waist—29 ins. divided by 4 is 7¼ ins. plus 1 inch for seams = 8¼ ins. × 5 sts. to the inch, or 42 sts., even number.
2. Hips—39 ins. plus 4 ins. = 43 ins., divided by 4 is 10¾ ins., plus 1 inch for seams is 11¾ ins. × 5 sts. to the inch, is 60 sts., even number.
3. Width at the Bottom—43 ins. plus 10 ins. = 53 ins., divided by 4 = 13¼, plus 1 inch equals 14¼ ins. × 5 sts. to the inch or 72 sts.
   Diagrams 146 and 147 are self-explanatory.

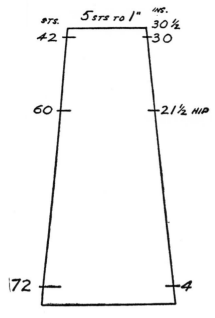

STS.   5 STS TO 1"   INS.

42   30½ 30

60   21½ HIP

72   4

DIAGRAM 146.

ins

last ½ inch even

42 sts	30½	
	30	
	29½	
	28½	
	27½	
	26½	
	25½	
	24½	
	23½	
	22½	
60 sts	21½	hip
	19½	
	15½	
	12	
	8	
72 sts	4	

DIAGRAM 147.

CHAPTER 40

FITTED JACKETS

DIFFERENCES IN MEASUREMENTS FROM SWEATERS AND BLOUSES

	Sweater	*Jacket*
Waist	28 inches	plus 2 inches = 30 inches
Across Back	17½ "	plus 1 inch = 18½ "
Front Bust	18½ "	plus 1 inch = 19½ "
Underarm-to-Waist	8 "	minus ½ inch = 7½ "
Shoulder-to-Shoulder	14½ "	plus 1 inch = 15½ "
Sleeve Underarm Length	17½ "	minus ½ inch = 17 "
Wrist	6 "	same
Upperarm	11 "	same
Armscye	19 "	plus 1 inch = 20 inches

CHAPTER 41

FITTED JACKETS—DARTS

Measurements

BACK

½ Waist—15 inches
Across Back Underarm—20 inches
Across Front Bust—22 inches
Shoulder-to-Shoulder—15½ inches
Underarm-to-Waist—8 inches
Waist to Hip—17½ inches, 5 inches down
Stitch Gauge—7 sts. to the inch

Method

1. Hips—17½ ins. × 7 sts. to the inch = 124 sts.
2. Waist—15 ins. × 7 sts. to the inch = 104 sts.
3. Across Back Underarm—20 ins. × 7 sts. to the inch = 140 sts.

4. Shoulder-to-Shoulder—15½ inches × 7 sts. to the inch = 108 sts.

5. Decreases and Increases

   (a) Bottom to Waist—124 sts. minus 104 sts. leaves 20 sts., 10 sts. at each side to decrease every ½ inch.

   (b) Waist-to-Underarm—140 sts. minus 104 sts. leaves 36 sts. Increase 8 sts. in each dart, 2 sts. at a time, every 1½ ins.; 4 times, making 16 sts.; and 10 times, every ¾ inch at the sides for a total of 36 sts. See diagram 148.

   (c) Underarm-to-Shoulder—15½ ins. × 7 = 108 sts. 140 sts. minus 108 sts. leaves 32 sts., 16 at each side.

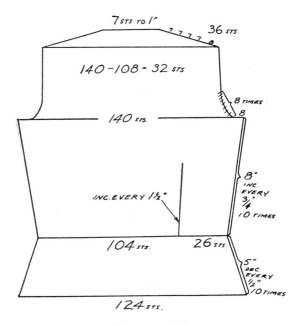

DIAGRAM 148.

FRONT

The sides are shaped the same as the back, and there are the same number of shoulder stitches.

Measurements

Across Front Bust—22 inches; ½ is 11 inches × 7 sts. to the inch or 77 sts. (78 even number).

Note: No allowance has been made for overlap in front.

Method

Follow diagram.

1. 78 sts. minus 52 sts. leaves 26 sts. 10 decreases and 10 increases at the side to match the back shaping; therefore, 16 sts. to be increased in a dart.
2. Place a marker at ½ the waist, 26 sts., then increase before and after the marker, every ¾ inch, 8 times, as follows: Knit 24 sts., increase in a stitch, K. 1, marker, K. 1, increase in a stitch, and so on.
3. Shoulder Dart
    As 18 sts. is the center of the shoulder, and 8 stitches have to be decreased in a dart, begin 5 ins. below the tip of the shoulder, and decrease every inch, 4 times, as follows: K. 19, K. 2 together, K. 1, marker, K. 1, K. 2 together.

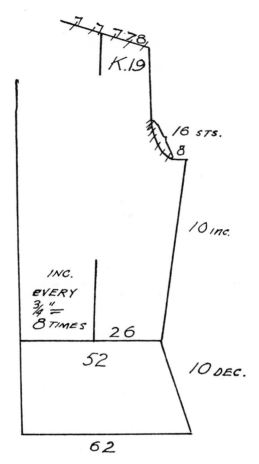

DIAGRAM 149.

CHAPTER 43

RAGLANS WITH SET-IN SLEEVES

Diagrams are self-explanatory.

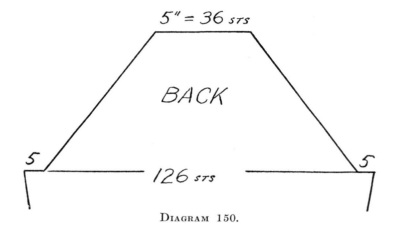

5" = 36 STS

BACK

5

5

126 STS

DIAGRAM 150.

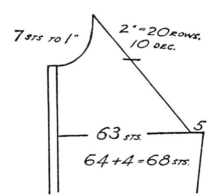

7 STS TO 1"

2" = 20 ROWS.
10 DEC.

63 STS.

5

64 + 4 = 68 STS.

DIAGRAM 151.

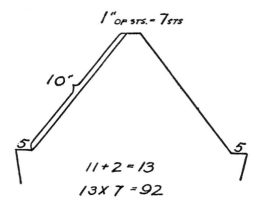

DIAGRAM 152.

CHAPTER 44

LONG DOLMAN SLEEVE

Measurements

Underarm to Waist—8 ins. minus 3 ins. leaves 5 inches.

Sleeve Underarm Length—18 inches minus 3 inches leaves 15 inches.

Shoulder stitches the same as for set-in sleeve.

Stitch Gauge—6 sts. to the inch.

Method

1. Add 1 inch of stitches, 1 stitch at a time, every other row, at the underarm, i.e., 6 sts.
2. Add 2 ins. of sts., ½ an inch at a time, i.e., 3 sts., every other row.
3. 15 ins. × 6 sts. to the inch = 90 sts. to add all at one time.
4. Knit even the desired ½ width of the cuff, 3½ ins.
5. Bind off ½ an inch of sts., 3 sts., every other row, for ½ the length of the sleeve, 7½ ins., = 45 sts.
6. Bind off 1 inch of sts., 6 sts., until the shoulder sts. remain.
7. Shape the shoulder.

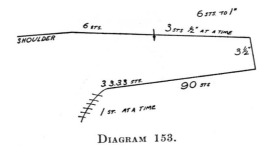

DIAGRAM 153.

CHAPTER 45

SHORTIE COATS

BOX COAT

Measurements

Across the Back Underarm—22 inches
Front Bust—12 inches for each front
Armscye—20 inches
Shoulder-to-Shoulder—15½ inches
Length from Underarm—14 inches
Sleeve—14 inches
Stitch Gauge—7 stitches to the inch

BACK

Method

1. 22 ins. $\times$ 7 sts. to the inch $=$ 154 sts. for 14 ins.
2. As 2 ins. in width were added across the back, the 2 inches of stitches is reduced in darts at the shoulders. See diagram.
3. Bind off 8 sts. at the armscye, then knit 2 together, 7 times, so 16 sts. remain for the darts, 8 for each shoulder.

FRONT

1. 12 ins. × 7 sts. to the inch = 84 sts. plus 6 sts. for the overlap = 90 sts. Knit even for 14 inches.
2. Armscye same as the back.
3. 2 ins. taken off in dart, 14 sts., 2 at a time, starting 6 ins. from the tip of the shoulder, every ¾ of an inch. See diagrams 154 and 155.

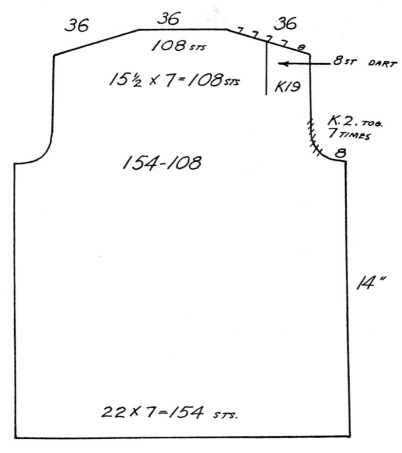

Diagram 154.

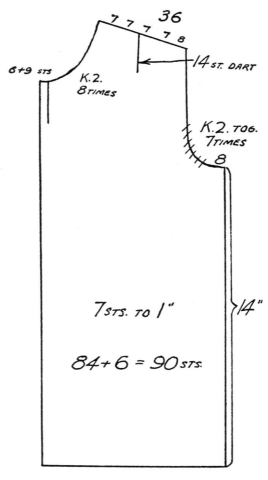

DIAGRAM 155.

SLEEVE

Diagram is self-explanatory.

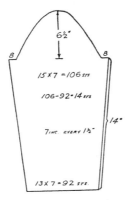

DIAGRAM 156.

CHAPTER 47

CHILDREN'S KNITTED WEAR

1. SKIRT OF STOCKINETTE STITCH

Measurements

Waist—24 inches
Length—19 inches
Width at the Bottom—48 inches.
Stitch Gauge—6 sts. to the inch

Method

1. 48 ins. × 6 sts. to the inch = 288 sts.; use 290 sts.
2. 24 ins. × 6 sts. to the inch = 144 sts.; use 140 sts.

3. 290 sts. minus 140 sts. leaves 150 sts. to decrease, i.e., 7 decreases of 20 sts., and 1 decrease of 10 sts. See diagram 157.

sts		ins	
		19	last in
140	K.6 (7.8)	18	
160		17	
		16	
		14	
		12	
		10	
		8	
260	K.12 (13.14)	6	
280	K.27 (28.29)	3	
290 sts			

DIAGRAM 157.

2. PLEATED SKIRT

Width at the Bottom—52 ins. and pleats 3 ins. wide.
Stitch Gauge—6 sts. to the inch

		Ins	
		19	
144 sts	K.8.P.8	18	
		17	
	10 decreases in	16	
	each rib	14	
		12	
		10	
		8	
		6	
		4	
		2	
324 sts	K.18.P.18		

DIAGRAM 158.

Method

1. Pleats 3 ins. wide—3 × 6 sts. to the inch = 18 sts. K. 18, P. 18 is 36 sts.
2. Width at the Bottom—52 ins. × 6 sts. to the inch = 312 sts.; use 324 sts. to be divisible by 36 sts. 36 into 324 goes 9, so 9 ribs of K. 18 and P. 18.
3. Width at the Waist—24 ins. × 6 sts. to the inch = 144 sts. 18 into 144 goes 8 times, so there are K. 8, P. 8 at the waist.

Comprehensive Index

KNIT TO FIT

HAND AND MACHINE KNITTING

COMPREHENSIVE INDEX

SWEATERS (*Continued*)
  working from the top down, 35-36
  Fronts
    bands, 48-49
    how to figure number of stitches, 48
    position of buttonholes, 48
    position of pockets, 49-51
    slipover and cardigan, 48
    zippers, 49
  Necklines—hand and machine
    cardigan, 53-57
    high round, 56-57
    how to figure, 53-57
    how to measure position, 53
    slipover with opening, 53-54
    slipover without opening, 54-55
    square neckline, 60
    "V" neckline, 58-60
  Sleeves
    caps of, 64
    child's sleeve, 63
    essentials of, 61
    long sleeves, 63
    man's sleeve, 63
    method of shaping, 61
    necessary extra widths, 61-63
    short sleeves, 65-66
    three-quarter length, 66
    to start from the top, 65